WITHDRAWN

D0073260

Unfounded Fears

Recent Titles in Contributions in Legal Studies

342.029
W388u

UNFOUNDED FEARS
Myths and Realities of a Constitutional Convention

Paul J. Weber & Barbara A. Perry
Foreword by HENRY J. ABRAHAM

CONTRIBUTIONS IN LEGAL STUDIES, NUMBER 55
Paul L. Murphy, *Series Editor*

GREENWOOD PRESS
NEW YORK • WESTPORT, CONNECTICUT • LONDON

Library of Congress Cataloging-in-Publication Data

Weber, Paul J.
   Unfounded fears : myths and realities of a constitutional
convention / Paul J. Weber and Barbara A. Perry ; foreword by Henry J.
Abraham.
     p.   cm.—(Contributions in legal studies, ISSN 0147–1074   ;
no. 55)
     Bibliography: p.
     Includes index.
     ISBN 0–313–26717–0 (lib. bdg. : alk. paper)
     1. Constitutional conventions—United States—History.   2. United
States—Constitutional history.   I. Perry, Barbara A.
II. Title. III. Series.
   KF4555.W43   1989
   342.73′0292—dc20
   [347.302292]   89–7502

British Library Cataloguing in Publication Data is available.

Copyright © 1989 by Paul J. Weber and Barbara A. Perry

All rights reserved. No portion of this book may be
reproduced, by any process or technique, without the
express written consent of the publisher.

A paperback edition of *Unfounded Fears: Myths and Realities of a Constitutional
Convention* is available from Praeger Publishers; ISBN: 0–275–93347–4.

Library of Congress Catalog Card Number: 89–7502
ISBN: 0–313–26717–0

First published in 1989

Greenwood Press, Inc.
88 Post Road West, Westport, Connecticut 06881

Printed in the United States of America

∞

The paper used in this book complies with the
Permanent Paper Standard issued by the National
Information Standards Organization (Z39.48–1984).

10 9 8 7 6 5 4 3 2 1

Copyright Acknowledgment

The authors express their gratitude to the publishers for permission to reprint
Paul J. Weber, "The Constitutional Convention: A Safe Political Option," *The
Journal of Law and Politics*, vol. 3, no. 1 (Winter 1986); Paul J. Weber, "Madi-
son's Opposition to a Second Convention," *Polity*, vol. 20, no. 3, (Spring 1988).

CONTENTS

ALLEGHENY COLLEGE LIBRARY

89-5237

FOREWORD

THE YEARS OF the U.S. Bicentennial constitute an appropriate period of time, indeed, to reflect upon that totally neglected, and all but mysterious if not mystic, mode of amending our Constitution, namely, the Constitutional Convention. Although twenty-six amendments have been adopted to the basic document—the last one in 1971, according the right to vote at the age of eighteen to all citizens of the United States—not one of those twenty-six became law by virtue of the "convention method." Yet the latter comprises one of the two mechanisms demonstrably available under Article V of the Constitution's text. It may thus be triggered if, upon the application of the legislatures of two-thirds of the now fifty states—i.e., thirty-four—Congress, in the words of the mandate, "shall call a Convention for proposing Amendments." Any such proposals would then become part and parcel of the Constitution "when ratified by the Legislatures of three-fourths of the several States, or by Convention in three-fourths thereof," with Congress determining upon either of those two available modes.

But despite its patent availability and attractiveness as an amending tool, its utilization has remained a theoretical rather than an actual one. Since the birth of our Republic in 1789, under the Constitution—itself the product of a constitutional convention, which some have regarded and still regard, albeit arguably, as a "runaway" convention—there have been more than 400 formal calls by state legislatures for a convention under Article V, including at least one from every state! One currently on the public agenda is the much-discussed (and much mis- and mal-analyzed) Balanced Budget Amendment, which (as of fall 1989) lacks the votes of only two states to activate the putative congressional call—a call that in all probability will not be issued.

Why the latter is a fairly safe guess—by one who never bets and is ever loath to venture prediction in matters governmental—is just one of several evaluative explications rendered with both expertise and sophistication by Professors Weber and Perry, whom I am proud to call both students and colleagues. They address in a lucid, informative, appealing, no-nonsense mode the vagaries and voodoos perpetrated and propounded both by proponents and opponents of the convention method, centering upon its substantive fears as well as its procedural intricacies. Only professionals of their ability, reflectiveness, and research experience in the matter can thus confidently term the constitutional convention "a safe political option," and they do so convincingly. It is comforting to perceive how the political genius of the Founding Fathers once again provides proof positive as a firmament upon which the contemporary political process can lean and adapt the "felt necessities" of the system.

Such "leaning" requires positive leadership, but it also demands involvement by that all-too-often reluctant dragon, the public at large, whose love for the Constitution is a constant but whose "scienter" of its contents—even of its significance—is frequently alarmingly deficient. If the constitutional-convention mode of constitutional amendment is to become reality—as the authors of this important book not only hope but advocate as a fundamental element of American democracy, a democratic cure for democratic ills—the public must become infinitely more involved in the affairs of state than it has evinced contemporarily. Not even fifty percent of the electorate bothered to vote in the most recent (1988) presidential election, a participatory low that unhappily constitutes not the exception but the norm. The ancient Greeks had a word, *idiotēs* ("idiot"), for the man who took no part or interest in civic matters, which carried the social and political connotation of paying no attention to the state and the community but simply tending to private affairs. In the words of the sage Pericles in the celebrated Funeral Oration: "We regard a man who takes no interest in public life not as a harmless but as a useless character."

In his *Politics*, Aristotle defined a citizen as one "who has the power to take part in the deliberative or judicial administration of any state." Becoming involved in the constitutional-convention option could well serve to lift significant components of our citizenry from the *idiotēs* status to that of democratic participation in the potentially fascinating democratic process. As Professors Weber and Perry point out so persuasively, the "dangers" present in the option are frequently visionary or self-serving. The built-in safeguards, direct as well as indirect, are as genuine as they are apposite. The pleas to employ the convention method have much to commend them. The unlikelihood of runaway conventions is self-evident. Whatever the realistic prognosis of the fashioning and adopting of an amendment via the convention method may in fact be—it is a dim one—the democratic process has much to gain and little, if anything, to lose by embracing it.

Henry J. Abraham
James Hart Professor of Government and Foreign Affairs
University of Virginia
Charlottesville
Fall 1989

1

INTRODUCTION

THIS BOOK REALLY began in a seminar at the Brookings Institution during the summer of 1982 sponsored by Project 87, a bicentennial effort planned jointly by the American Political Science Association and the American Historical Association. The seminar was led by Professor Henry Abraham, who sparked a revolt in one of the authors of this book with a perhaps too cavalier remark about the dangers of a second constitutional convention. In the discussion that followed, Professor Abraham observed that very little dispassionate research had been done on the topic and thought it worth pursuing. What eventually became Chapter 6 was originally presented as a paper at a Southern Political Science Association panel on which sat Professors Kermit Hall of the University of Florida and Walter Dellinger of Duke Law School. Both disagreed vigorously with the thesis of the paper, while urging further research and offering numerous helpful suggestions.

Phase two began at a similar institute, this one at Columbia University, hosted by Professor Richard Morris, who at eighty-two was a most delightful and intellectually challenging historian. That seminar on the Founding Period of the American Republic inspired the ideas for Chapters 2 and 3.

Next came one of those fortuitous events that occasionally thrusts scholars into the unfamiliar world of practical politics, a phone call from David Keating, executive director of the National Taxpayers Union, the group most responsible for the current drive for a balanced budget amendment. Keating had read the paper from the Southern Political Science Association and wondered if its author would be willing to testify before state legislatures about the safety of the proposed constitutional convention. This presented something of a dilemma, since we were most undecided about the need for a balanced budget amendment. An agreement was reached whereby testimony would focus only on the safety of a convention, not on the merits of a balanced budget amendment.

Testifying before the Connecticut, Michigan, and Kentucky legislatures was an eye-opening experience. Academic debate and polite intellectual disagreements were replaced by brute power politics: clever slogans, pious rhetoric, interest-group turnout, scare tactics, and, above all, vote counts. Few knew, and even fewer cared, about the historical record of convention calls or experience. There was no room here for nuance or thoughtfully constructed arguments. It was a fascinating introduction to practical politics, and out of this experience grew Chapters 4 and 5. We knew as we were writing the book that eventually we would need to deal directly with our ambivalence about a balanced budget amendment, since it is still the most salient issue for which a convention could be called. The result is Chapter 7.

Having traced the genesis of the book, it may be helpful to the reader if we spell out our purpose in writing it, since we do not fit into any of the traditional "camps." Although we do not support the call for a balanced budget amendment (at least not yet) and are not in favor of calling a constitutional convention for any of the other reasons currently in vogue—i.e., to allow common prayer in the public schools, to establish the rights of the unborn, or to outlaw busing to achieve racial integration— we *do* wish to defend the intellectual credibility and political possibility of calling a convention if and when a situation arises when it would be appropriate.

Perhaps such a purpose is quixotic, but we rather think of it as having several long-term values. First, the prospect of calling a second constitutional convention has already proved useful in the past as a "threat" to Congress, forcing it to act. One thinks immediately of the Seventeenth Amendment, providing for the direct election of Senators. Only the threat of a convention forced a reluctant Senate to approve the amendment. On several other occasions, including the current budgetary difficulties, calls for a convention have forced Congress to take the issue seriously and seek a solution. Such calls have been instrumental in raising public consciousness about the issues and have increased the pressure on politicians to propose remedies. To be useful such threats must be credible, and to be credible a convention must be recognized as a possible and safe political option.

Second, and perhaps even more quixotic, we believe the convention option useful to protect our republican form of government. A certain amount of contemporary literature points out the immense difficulty of unseating incumbent members of Congress. If the trend toward PAC financing of elections continues, our legislators will become increasingly less responsible to their geographic constituents, more able to protect their own political careers with the help of wealthy contributors, and less amenable to political reform. The convention option can be a way to encourage reforms or make them if necessary.

Third, as our research progressed and as one of the authors participated in the debates in the state legislatures, we became increasingly less comfortable with the myths underlying much of the discussion, specifically, that the first Convention ran away and that Madison was implacably opposed to a second one. By myths we mean assertions taken as truth without examination or nuance. This, too, may be quixotic, but we think it important in this time of bicentennial celebrations to provide and flesh out a context within which to examine the actions of the Founders. In a time of cynicism and disbelief we believe it important to defend the wisdom, honesty, and carefulness of the Founders when they wrote and ratified the Constitution. These reasons prompted us to write this book.

No doubt critics will harbor a nagging suspicion that somehow we have a hidden agenda and that secretly we want a constitutional convention. Although we must admit that such an event would likely draw attention to what is otherwise destined to be just another scholarly volume, and although we would enjoy being invited to talk shows to comment about such a unique occurrence, when all is said and done, we do not favor calling a convention. We prefer to reserve that option for what Madison called "great and extraordinary occasions." Calling and holding a convention would be a costly and time-consuming process and the possibility should be reserved for those moments in history when we have exhausted other less cumbersome alternatives.

With these preliminaries out of the way, we turn to a summary of the individual chapters. Chapter 1 confronts the issue of whether the First Convention, held in 1787, actually ran away. Common wisdom holds that it did. We believe the issue is more complex. Literalists who insist on focusing their attention exclusively on the words of the Confederate Congress, which called a convention for "the sole and express purpose of revising the Articles of Confederation," and who close their minds to any consideration of context and intention, might do well to skip this chapter. We look first at the declining fortunes of the Confederacy and the growing despair of many of its national leaders over the institutional and structural infirmities of government under the Articles of Confederation. Clearly something had to be done, but did the Founders have the authority to do so much or to replace one constitution with another?

To answer that question we look to the process by which the Convention was called. We show that from the outset it was a political rather than a legal act. The Articles made no provision for a convention, and that from the very beginning there were no illusions among either proponents or opponents. Both understood that an effort was being made to forge a stronger central government at the expense of state sovereignty. The differences between the two groups, soon to be called Federalists and Antifederalists, can be seen in reading the parts of the call by Congress for the convention they believed to be controlling. Whereas the Antifederalists (and those who today insist that the first convention ran away) stressed those words quoted in the above paragraph, the Federalists thought that the controlling part of the call was the passage that stated its purpose, namely, "to render the federal constitution adequate to the exigencies of government and the preservation of the union."

Finally, we argue, primarily because it is little known today, that the Founders thought, talked, and wrote a great deal both during and after the Convention about the legitimacy of their actions. They were aware that they had gone beyond the literal mandate of the convention call and that they needed to justify their actions. Although we have attached Madison's major defense, written in Federalist #40, as Appendix I, we can summarize their argument here in three steps: (1) the need to do what was necessary to preserve the union, (2) the Articles of Confederation proved so inadequate that it would be better to start over and build on other fundamental principles, and (3) ultimately all they could do was to propose the changes and leave it up to the people to accept or reject them.

In Chapter 2 we address a myth hardly less pervasive, namely, that James Madison, who so ardently pressed for convening the first convention, stood with equal passion against ever convening another. Indeed, it was Madison who wrote, "Having witnessed the difficulties and dangers experienced by the first Convention . . . I should tremble for the result of a Second." Although much has been made of Madison's remark by opponents of a present-day convention, a review of the context provides balance and nuance. We show first that in the letter containing the above sentence Madison was fighting a tactic of those who opposed the constitution written in 1787. Frustrated by their inability to stop state conventions from ratifying the new document, Patrick Henry of Virginia and George Clinton of New York hit upon the idea of having state conventions call for a second convention *before* the first was ratified, ostensibly in order to add a Bill of Rights and make other changes the states might wish.

Madison knew that such a convention would sabotage the work done in the first. He wanted to give the new constitution a chance to work, then make changes as necessary. We liken his stand on another convention to his opposition to a Bill of Rights. He was not opposed to either in principle; he simply did not think either was necessary at the time, and if not well executed could cause more harm than good. On the other hand, we do not go so far in this chapter as to try to project what Madison might think about a contemporary call except to point out that the intervening years have provided what he found lacking in 1788. This consists of a time of trial to discover what would work and what wouldn't under a new constitution, a tradition of loyalty to constitutional values, and stable mechanisms by which to resolve the technical difficulties of calling and conducting a convention.

In Chapter 5 we review the "other" experience with conventions, those on the state level, to see what they might teach us about a possible national convention. In one respect, with more than 230 conventions, states have provided a wealth of practical experience. There is a major difference that limits what can be learned; that difference is federalism. States do not have to have their amendments approved by forty-nine other states, and hence do not face the variety of groups and interests that exist on the national level. Despite that limitation, we trace the lessons we believe can be learned from state conventions. We purposely use this chapter to confront many of the questions that are raised about a potential convention, such as the role of the judiciary, what happens in the event of legislative recalcitrance, the possibility of limiting a convention, the process for electing delegates, what kinds of people tend to get elected, the ability of the legislature to establish and control the procedures and substance of what a convention does, and even such mundane issues as public hearings, committee structures, and rigidity of convention rules. These technicalities concerned Madison and still trouble many modern opponents of a convention. Our review shows that mistakes can be (and have been) made, but they are not inevitable, and experience on the state level provides many potential answers to the technical questions.

It is remarkable that despite more than 400 applications, no constitutional convention has been called since 1787. Given that the early effort to derail ratification of the first constitution through the tactic of calling for a second and that the convention option is far less efficient than having Congress propose amendments, perhaps this failure should be no surprise after all. Nevertheless, in Chapter 4 we review the applications as closely as historical records allow, to determine the types of issues that triggered calls. Several intriguing patterns emerge. In the first century following ratification, the few petitions to Congress were for general conventions to address contemporary constitutional crises, namely nullification and the impending Civil War. For reasons we discuss in the chapter, calls in the next century were primarily for limited conventions. Early calls were for such things as the popular election of Senators, outlawing polygamy, prohibition of alcoholic beverages, and repeal of the income tax.

Current liberal aversion to convention calls, however, is entirely understandable. Since the 1950s applications have come almost exclusively from conservatives outraged by the liberal activism of the Warren Court. Integration of schools, reapportionment, and school prayer started the surge of petitions. Later issues arose from the liberal decisions of the Burger Court, abortion and busing, and the expansive spending of a Democratic-controlled Congress.

In Chapter 6 we confront directly the central question for a second convention. Would a constitutional convention be politically safe? Could a convention called for a limited purpose be trusted not to run away? Our answer is a resounding yes, probably more convincing to us than to critics of a convention. Myths die slow deaths. Essentially our argument is that efforts to find legal safeguards are misplaced; what we have are a series of *political* safeguards. Because there has never been a successful convention call, we have had to abandon our historical methodology for this chapter and take up a tool we call political inference. We show that, based on established practices and patterns in American politics, at each of the six steps in the process of calling and conducting a convention and getting an amendment ratified, there are built-in political safeguards.

Our conclusions are that a convention would be as safe as any other political process in the United States, and that far from being a reckless alternative to congressional proposals of amendments, it is an option less prone to errors made in haste or the heat of interest-group pressures. As we try to show, for an amendment to run the convention gauntlet successfully, it must have the backing not only of a majority or a powerful elite, but of a consensus of the population.

Stage one is the need to garner applications for a convention from two-thirds of the state legislatures. Since 1789 no convention call has overcome this hurdle.

Stage two is the process of having Congress call the convention. This is a twofold safeguard in that Congress can establish convention procedures and the Supreme Court can rule on the inevitable legal challenges to such procedures.

Stage three is the election of delegates. We look at American electoral history to see who runs in elections and who wins, and argue that convention delegates will mirror current distribution among parties and ideological groups, hardly a radical or irresponsible crowd.

Stage four is the convention itself. Granted the type of delegates elected, media attention, the number of and divisions among delegates, the delegates' awareness that their proposals must be presented to Congress, and the need to get proposed amendments ratified, it would be extraordinarily difficult for one faction or a radical position to prevail.

Stage five is the role of Congress when the work of a convention is presented to it. If the convention went beyond its mandate, Congress would refuse to forward the results to the states. Again, a court challenge would follow, and the court would perform its guardian role once more.

Stage six is ratification. Assuming, for the sake of argument, failure at all the previous stages, a proposed amendment must now be ratified by thirty-eight states—four more than were needed to propose it! At this stage one can anticipate media, interest groups, and public involvement, presidential efforts to influence the outcome, and additional court challenges. Even the time involved in moving through the six stages is insurance against hasty or ill-conceived amendments. In sum, one can hardly think of a safer political process, Chapter 6 spells out each of these arguments in detail.

As a case study of a convention movement, Chapter 7 begins by sketching the history of the balanced budget campaign and then presents the major arguments for and against the amendment. On balance we find the latter arguments more plausible. Economist Paul Samuelson argues convincingly that there are no inherent flaws in the *constitutional* structure that cause the deficits. Rather, the difficulties arise from a lack of consensus among voters that the problem is serious enough to be solved and a lack of political will among their representatives. We see these as *political* problems with *political* solutions.

Despite our intense study of the issue, we are not certain an amendment would work. Would more expenditures simply move "off-budget"? Would Congress engage in other legal sleight-of-hand reminiscent of Kentucky's famed "rubber dollar"? And if an amendment had sufficient rigidity to work, would such rigidity lead to more severe economic difficulties that we experience under even a massive deficit? Finally, we share with many political scientists a belief that the Constitution, as the fundamental law of the land, will remain strongest if amendments are reserved for solving structural problems and protecting or expanding individual liberties. This is not to say we oppose dealing with all fiscal issues via amendment. We argue only that this is not the proper time or proper amendment. Proposals for a line-item veto, for example, would open up whole new areas for discussion.

Such is the book. In closing this introduction there is one topic for which we found no "quite right" place in the chapters, but which we wish to address briefly here, namely, the opposition of several religious interest groups to any constitutional convention. Groups leading the opposition are Americans United, the Baptist Joint Committee, Seventh-Day Adventists, and, as far as we can determine, several local chapters of the American Jewish Congress. Opposition began among these groups in the 1960s in response to a fundamentalist effort to overturn Supreme Court decisions outlawing state-sponsored prayer in public schools. Since then these groups have opposed all convention calls for whatever purpose, based on the fear that any convention, once assembled, could abolish or rewrite the First Amendment. The authors share a deeply rooted commitment to religious liberty and find this opposition ironic, since it was only the threat of a second convention that forced Madison to submit a Bill of Rights to Congress. Without the threat of a second convention, there would have been no First Amendment.

We hope the book demonstrates, particularly in Chapter 6,

that such fears are unfounded. However, religious groups have raised a problem we do not directly address elsewhere. Religious fears are not that a minority could capture a convention but that a majority could, and thereby impose some common religious dogma or creed, or at least remove the protective cover of the First Amendment. Our response is threefold: (1) a convention can do no more than Congress can currently do, that is, propose amendments; vigilance is always necessary, but the dangers to religious liberty from a convention are no more than those posed by Congress; (2) even a substantial majority in a convention is not enough to pose a threat to religious liberty; it would take a consensus spread out over time, geography, ideology, and several political institutions, i.e., more of a consensus than it would take to accomplish the same ends by less visible means; and (3) a majority of American citizens, however it might be constituted, are committed to the protection of minority rights. A convention is no more likely to bring oppression than is any other institution in American politics.

It might be well to note here that authority for a constitutional convention arises from Article V of the Constitution, which reads:

The Congress, whenever two-thirds of both Houses shall deem it necessary, shall propose Amendments to this Constitution, or, on the Application of the Legislatures of two-thirds of the several States, shall call a Convention for proposing Amendments, which, in either Case, shall be valid to all Intents and Purposes, as part of this Constitution, when ratified by the Legislatures of three-fourths of the several States, or by Conventions in three-fourths thereof, as the one or the other Mode of Ratification may be proposed by the Congress.

We wish to thank the many people who have helped in the preparation and writing of this book: Professor Henry Abraham for his initial inspiration and his kindness in writing the Foreword, Mr. David Keating of the National Taxpayers Union for the opportunity to testify before several state legislatures, our colleagues Professors Mary Hawkesworth, Joel Goldstein, and Landis Jones for their suggestions and criticisms, our families for their encouragement, Sandy Hartz and Laura Abell who did a super job in typing the manuscript, and especially Mildred Vasan of Greenwood Press for her good nature and trust that we could get the manuscript completed, if not quite by the contractual deadline.

2

DID THE FIRST CONVENTION RUN AWAY?

There are great seasons when persons with limited powers are justified in exceeding them, and a person would be contemptible not to risk it.

—Edmund Randolph, June 16, 1787

AMONG THOSE WHO oppose calling a second convention, one of the most telling arguments is that "we called one convention and it ran away!" The implication is that a second convention might very well do the same. What appears to be a truism bears a closer look, if only to establish that what the Founders did was far more cautious, careful, and respectful of citizens' rights and established procedures than the term "runaway convention" implies.

The purpose of this chapter is to demonstrate that the Founders were very sensitive to challenges to the legality of their action and made every effort to establish both themselves and their process as legitimate. They were neither reckless revolutionaries nor cynical power seekers. A few reflections on the meaning of the term "runaway convention" may be a useful way to set the stage for a discussion of the historical record.

The phrase "runaway convention" is rhetorically appealing because it implies an unquestioned truth and yet is so conveniently vague that it cannot be either proved or disproved. If by the term one means that the Founders called a convention for one public reason while having a hidden agenda, such as a couple who announce to their parents that they are going to a movie, then run away to get married, clearly the convention did not run away. If one means that a convention called for a particular purpose suddenly careened out of control with no particular destination in mind, like a carriage horse that suddenly feels the power of the bit between his teeth, again, the Convention did not run away.

Commentators usually lack such imagination and restrict themselves to the argument that the Confederate Congress explicitly called a convention for *"the sole and express purpose of revising the Articles of the Confederation* and reporting to Congress and the several legislatures such alterations and provisions therein as shall, when agreed to in Congress and confirmed by the States, render the federal constitution adequate to the exigencies of government and the preservation of the union"[1] (emphasis added). Seen from this limited perspective it can indeed be argued that the convention did "run away."

But the perspective is far too narrow to reflect reality adequately. The vision of the Founders was far broader, and so should be the understanding of contemporary commentators. An analogy may help make the point. Imagine that a person convicted of a crime is sentenced to home incarceration and legally prohibited from leaving his premises for thirty days. On the fifteenth day the building catches fire. The prisoner flees his apartment and walks to the nearest police station. Has he violated the terms of his sentence? In a narrow sense he has. Was he justified in doing so? That was the dilemma the Founders faced. For James Madison and his allies, the choice was between legality and survival. In the following pages we trace the efforts they made to resolve that dilemma.

LIFE UNDER THE ARTICLES OF CONFEDERATION

Americans who challenge the legality of the first Constitutional Convention rarely question the right of the Confederate

Congress to govern, but there is a legitimate question here. Americans by a simple fiat declared themselves free of Great Britain in July 1776. By what right? The Declaration of Independence was an enormously persuasive piece of rhetoric attempting to justify an illegal act by appealing to a higher legitimacy. Over a year later, in November 1777, the Continental Congress, a loose coordinating body attempting to finance and direct the Revolutionary War effort, submitted to all the state legislatures a copy of the Articles of Confederation. Once ratified, the Articles were to be the legal foundation for the new republic. It was not until May 1781 that the last state approved the Articles and the entity to be called "The United States of America" was formed.

Did this action of the Continental Congress and the several state legislatures establish a "legal" state? Certainly not from the British perspective and not according to the procedures recognized by any international law of the period. Nor was a popular vote ever taken. Even the Founders recognized the legal fragility of their creation. Although certainly not a disinterested party at the time, Alexander Hamilton's observations in *Federalist* No. 22 indicate this awareness:

It has not a little contributed to the infirmities of the existing federal system [i.e., under the Articles of Confederation] that it never had a ratification by the PEOPLE. Resting on no better foundation than the consent of the several legislatures it has been exposed to frequent and intricate questions concerning the validity of its powers, and had, in some instances, given birth to the erroneous doctrine of a right of legislative appeal.[2]

It was a scant six years later that the order calling a convention was issued by the Confederate Congress. Did the Congress even then have the right to meet, much less to call a convention? Some would argue that time itself, the treaty of peace with Great Britain, and in 1783 the acquiescence both of state legislatures and the people at large created a de facto legitimacy. The point we would add is that the concept of "legality" cannot be taken in too rigid or inflexible a sense.

But that leads to a second problem. If a government can gain

ALLEGHENY COLLEGE LIBRARY

legitimacy over time, can it also lose it? Certainly in the eyes of the American patriots, the British government of King George III had lost its right to rule. Most of the Declaration of Independence is devoted to listing the reasons for this loss of legitimacy. In a manuscript written during April 1787, the month preceding the convention, and now rarely read, James Madison spelled out the reasons why government under the Articles of Confederation had also lost its power to command obedience.[3] They are listed here without Madison's explanatory paragraphs:

1. Failure of the States to comply with the Constitutional Requisitions
2. Encroachment by the States on the Federal Authority
3. Violations of the Law of Nations and of Treaties
4. Trespasses of the States on the Rights of each other
5. Want of Concert in matters where common interest requires it
6. Want of Guaranty to the States of their Constitutions and Laws against internal violence
7. Want of sanction to the Laws and of Coercion in the Government of the Confederacy
8. Want of Ratification by the People of the Articles of Confederation
9. Multiplicity of Laws in the several States
10. Mutability of the Laws of the States
11. Injustice of the Laws of the States

Madison was not alone in his despair over government under the Articles of Confederation, and events appeared to bear out his pessimistic assessment. As one commentator writes,

Although it oversaw important accomplishments in the successful conclusion of the Revolutionary War and the organization of the Northwest Territories, it was, in a literal sense, constitutionally incapable of dealing adequately with the persistent problems facing the country. Any successful economic policy was precluded by the failure to give the Congress authority to tax, to regulate commerce or to control credit, and by an inability to deal with the delinquency of many

states in their financial contributions. With respect to international re-
lations, the central government was incompetent to establish national
tariff or trade policies and this resulted in a serious disadvantage in
competing or negotiating with other countries. Moreover, the state
governments, to which most important public decision-making had been
confided, were increasingly prone to inefficiency and corruption and,
consequently, to diminished public respect.[4]

Perhaps no one put it better than George Washington in a
letter to Thomas Jefferson on May 30, 1787:

> The business of this convention is as yet very much in embryo to
> form any opinion of the conclusion. Much is expected from it by some;
> not much by others; and nothing by a few. That something is neces-
> sary, none will deny; for the situation of the general government, if it
> can be called a government, is shaken to its foundation, and liable to
> be overturned by every blast. In a word, it is at an end; and unless a
> remedy is soon applied, anarchy and confusion will inevitably ensue.[5]

Whether Madison, Washington, and other Federalists were
correct in their gloomy assessment of government under the
Articles has been the subject of some dispute,[6] but it seems clear
that they *thought* they were correct in viewing the Articles as
politically bankrupt. That created the sense of urgency that they
sought to replace.

A third and related problem was that the national government under the Articles appeared in 1786 to be winding down.
Quorums in Congress were difficult to muster and more difficult to maintain. Reports were written and debated but action
rarely taken. With the exception of one high point in 1787 when
Congress passed the Northwest Ordinance, there appears to have
been a steady decline in attendance, interest, activity, and morale. "By 1785 the government of the United States was a
wheedling beggar. . . . The first constitution . . . went from
crisis to crisis and finally into a long slide toward death."[7]

The question in the minds of contemporaries who thought
of such things was not one of abandoning a status quo for gree-
ner pastures, but which path to take out of a system in the last
throes of disintegration. And there were options. Although some
"state's righters," soon to be known as Antifederalists, envi-

sioned a Balkan-like set of thirteen independent nations, they tended to be from the large states—New York, Pennsylvania, and Virginia—who recognized that they would soon dominate their entire regions and therefore had something to gain from disintegration. A more likely scenario was devolution into the three natural areas, South, Middle, and North, each developing its own particular form of government. But for a few at least, admittedly among the more affluent, educated elites, the vision of a united nation of the whole was something worth fighting for.

As Madison noted in a letter written in late February 1787: "The bulk of the people will probably prefer the lesser evil of a partition of the Union into three more practicable and energetic governments. The latter idea I find after long confinement to individual speculations and private circles, is beginning to show itself in the newspapers."[8]

The point of the discussion so far is that one should not make too much of the legitimacy of the Congress that called the convention, nor too little of the legitimacy of the Founders who went beyond the limits of that call. As we now try to show, those who shepherded the new constitution through the writing and ratification stages were as careful to establish legitimacy as had been those who created the Articles of Confederation.

Although both Hamilton and Madison mentioned the lack of popular ratification as undermining the legitimacy of government under the Articles, the major thrust of the Federalist argument was pragmatic: a republican form of government could not survive under the Articles. Some people predicted chaos, other tyranny. Once that specter was on the horizon, the Federalists in general and Madison in particular worked diligently to make needed changes. While they did not start off with a clear-cut idea of what was needed, neither were they willing to career heedlessly into reckless experimentation.

EFFORTS TO SOLVE THE PROBLEMS

From the beginning, government under the Articles had not worked well. As early as 1780, Alexander Hamilton, a precocious twenty-three-year-old, was pointing out the problems to his friend James Duane and raising the possibility of calling a convention to create the "solid coercive union" he thought necessary for survival. He even persuaded the New York legislature to propose that Congress call a Convention of the States to remedy the problems. In 1781 both Washington and Madison were pondering possible solutions. Washington alternately despaired and hoped at Mount Vernon; Madison attempted to work through Congress. Various reports attempting to solve problems piecemeal, financial proposals in 1781 and 1783, a navigation law in 1784, and a tax proposal in 1786 came to nothing. The very structure and voluntary composition of Congress insured the weakness of this so-called legal body.

Extralegal approaches fared better. Rankling problems between Virginia and Maryland over navigation on the Potomac prompted Washington to invite commissioners from the two states to meet at Mount Vernon to work out a plan for cooperation. Surprised by their own success, the states proposed a second meeting, this one to include first Pennsylvania and Delaware; then, as the idea gained momentum, all other states that cared to send delegates. The second meeting was to be held at Annapolis on the first Monday in September 1786.

By all objective measures, the meeting was a failure. Only five of the thirteen states bothered to send delegates. Hamilton, however, with the almost certain connivance of Madison, salvaged what respect he could and drafted a report to the five state legislatures calling on them to appoint delegates for yet another meeting "to meet in Philadelphia on the second Monday in May next" (1787),

to take into consideration the situation of the United States, to devise such further provisions as shall appear to them necessary to render the constitution of the federal government adequate to the exigencies of the Union; and to report such an act for that purpose to the United States in Congress assembled as, when agreed to by them and afterwards confirmed by the legislatures of every state, will effectually provide for the same.[9]

Whereas Hamilton's report was addressed only to the legislatures of the states that had sent delegates, its stated intent was obviously far broader than their respective boundaries, and "from motives of respect," as Hamilton quaintly put it, the report was sent to Congress and the other states as well.

Even then there was little hope. Why would delegates go to Philadelphia when they would not go to Annapolis? And why would Congress issue a call for a convention when the Annapolis report had not asked it to? And even if it did, under the urging of Madison, why would the reluctant states send delegates? The answers lie in several fortuitous circumstances. Foremost among these is surely Shay's Rebellion, which occurred after the Annapolis report was published and before Congress issued its call for a convention. An event profoundly more important in American history than Watergate or the Iran-Contra affair, Shay's was not so much a rebellion as a series of demonstrations and mass protests that eventually got out of hand when it appeared there was no police force or militia strong enough to resist. The demonstrators were in fact mostly debt-saddled farmers, many of them Revolutionary War veterans who had become increasingly disillusioned with the unwillingness of their state government to lower taxes or stimulate trade. Never particularly well led and without any long-term plans, the demonstrators finally were dispersed by the Massachusetts militia after a desultory attack on the Springfield arsenal.

Apparently what so unnerved state legislators was the popular support enjoyed by the demonstrators and the weakness of the legislators' ability to respond. Civil war in Massachusetts may well have been avoided by the courageous leadership of one man, General Benjamin Lincoln. It could have happened elsewhere just as easily, and state legislators from Connecticut to Georgia knew it. They also knew that the Revolutionary War had begun at Lexington and Concord, both in Massachusetts. Was this uprising a foretaste of things to come? Shay's Rebellion captured politicians' attention as no report ever could. When one reads the letters to and from members of the Continental Congress in February 1787, it is remarkable how often comments about "the recent events in Massachusetts" are followed by comments about a proposed convention.[10]

A second fortuitous circumstance was that seven of the states, a majority, simply appointed delegates to a convention without waiting for Congress.[11] Why did they do it? In one sense the question is probably more important to us than it was to the Founders. Beyond the obvious point just discussed, i.e., many of the elites believed the Confederation was in serious trouble, the truth is that legal formalities were far less settled than we would expect today; those in leadership positions in states corresponded with each other regularly and legislatures felt quite free to take independent action. What happened in this case was that, responding to the call from Annapolis, Governor Edmund Randolph of Virginia guided an act through the Virginia legislature calling for a convention and appointing delegates. He then sent a letter to the Continental Congress informing it of the action. *At the same time* he sent copies of the Virginia act to all the state governors. This stimulated similar action in six other state legislatures, which in turn put a good deal of pressure on Congress to respond in some way to Randolph's initiative.

A third fortuitous and increasingly unlikely event was the achievement of a quorum in Congress, a fact itself stimulated no doubt by Shay's Rebellion. (Perhaps one should also include here an improvement in Madison's health, which allowed him to exert his energy and influence to the extent that he was finally able to persuade Congress to pass its resolution of February 21 calling for a convention.) What is intriguing here is the ambiguity with which members responded to Randolph's letter and the reasons why two states originally opposed to any convention, New York and Massachusetts, agreed to call one and to appoint delegates.

In a letter of February 18, Madison spelled out the ambiguity: "A great disagreement of opinion exists as to the expediency of a recommendation from Congress to the backward states in favor of the meeting. It would seem as if some of the states disliked it because it is an extraconstitutional measure, and their dislike would be removed or lessened by a sanction from Congress to do it. On the other hand, it is suggested that some would dislike it the more if Congress should appear to interest themselves in it."[12] The problem, as he explained a few days later to Washington, was that members of Congress did not know whether their support would lend legitimacy to the convention or look like a power grab and therefore be a kiss of death.[13] What is clear is that members of Congress were quite aware of the "extralegality" of the push for a convention.

The agreement of New York and Massachusetts to support a convention call and send delegates is more difficult to explain. Perhaps it can be done only in terms of "luck" or fortuitous circumstances. New York politicians were divided into factions with the governorship in the hands of an ambitious but not entirely secure George Clinton. The convention call, now supported by a majority of states, posed something of a dilemma for Clinton. If he refused to cooperate and the other states went forward without New York, not only could they make changes in the Articles inimical to New York's interest (such as providing stronger protections for neighboring Connecticut, New Jersey, and the Vermont territory, which he hoped to acquire), but a successful convention might strengthen the nationalist faction in New York and lead to his own defeat. He could not run the risk.

Clinton's strategy was to support the call, then have the legislature appoint his own trusted supporters who could block any efforts to dilute New York's power. He was two-thirds successful. Of the three delegates selected, two, Robert Yates and John Lansing, never wavered in their opposition to the new Constitution. The third, Alexander Hamilton, was appointed as part of a legislative compromise and represented a strong nationalist position in the convention.

Massachusetts showed more uncertainty. The state legislature had sent a resolution to Congress two years earlier calling for a convention. At that time, two of its own delegates, Elbridge Gerry and Rufus King, responded negatively, warning of aristocratic attempts "to destroy republic institutions."[14] Now, after Shay's uprising, there was something of a change of heart. This is nowhere better expressed than in a letter from King to Gerry, both of whom would soon be delegates, February 18, 1787:

All the states south of this have appointed to the Convention, but the commissions, or authorities seem to be different. I say have appointed: five of them *have* appointed and the other three undoubtedly will appoint. I will not venture a conjecture relative to the policy of the measure in Massachusetts: the thing is so problematical, that I confess I am at some loss, I am rather inclined to the measure from an idea of prudence, or for the purpose of watching, than from an expectation that much Good will flow from it.[15]

What we can conclude from the discussion thus far is that the call to a convention came as no surprise to the various political groups and interests in 1787. It was the culmination of years of efforts by Federalists to resolve long-standing structural problems under the Articles of Confederation. Nor were there any illusions about the extralegal means of change a convention represented.

Unlike the situation two centuries later, there was no provision in the Articles for calling a convention. At the same time the convention call was not a revolution or coup d'état: it represented an enormous effort to stay within the mainstream, to maintain legitimacy. As Professor Richard Kay observes, "The extralegal character of the change was understood even prior to the convention and helps explain Congress' reluctance officially to initiate such an unorthodox technique of constitutional change."[16] In short, what the Federalists were trying to do was to effect major changes, impossible under the Articles, precisely *without* running away. This effort to mainstream legitimacy can also be seen as a thread woven through the convention itself.

A SEARCH FOR LEGITIMACY IN THE CONVENTION

The modern assumption that the Constitutional Convention "ran away" is somewhat ironic in light of the fact that this very issue was much debated—and ultimately resolved to their own satisfaction—by the members of the Convention itself. When Governor Randolph spelled out the Virginia Plan before the Convention on May 29, he quite clearly and consciously went beyond the congressional mandate, making only a half-hearted attempt to cast his plan as a revision of the Articles.[17] Charles Pinckney of South Carolina was quick to see the implications. "If the convention agreed to it [the Virginia Plan], it appeared

to him that their business was at an end; for as the powers of
the house in general were to revise the present confederation,
and to alter or amend it as the case might require; to determine
its [the Articles] insufficiency or incapacity of amendment or
improvement, must end in the dissolution of the powers [of the
Convention]."[18]

Madison remarks that this observation "had its weight"; certainly no one at the moment rose to refute Pinckney. In fact,
later the same day Elbridge Gerry objected to any distinction
being made between a federal and a national government, "for
if we do, it is questionable not only whether this convention can
propose a government totally different or whether Congress
itself would have a right to pass such a resolution as that before
the house." Again, there really was no answer.

It may be that the Federalists at first wished simply to ignore
a question they could not easily answer and hope that a discussion of the troubles of the Confederation and of the proposed
alterations would be sufficiently persuasive that the question
would simply go away. It was not to be that easy. Nonetheless,
the delegates did proceed to discuss a substantive issue, namely
the proposed composition of a national legislature.

The issue of the Convention's power surfaced again when
William Paterson proposed his New Jersey Plan. Small state
representatives were profoundly upset by Randolph's insistence
that the national legislature be elected on the basis of population, i.e., the larger the state the more representatives it would
have. Paterson reminded the delegates that the Constitutional
Convention was called as a result of an act of Congress and
needed to proceed on the basis of the Articles of Confederation, i.e., each state having an equal vote. If it did not, "we
should be charged by our constituents with usurpation."[19] Again,
there was no answer, as the delegates were floundering over
the most critical issue of the Convention—representation.

In a sense it seemed that the issue of the Convention's power
was not so much a sticking point as a debating point. Charles
Pinckney intimated as much when he pointed out that if New
Jersey were given an equal vote she would "dismiss her scruples
and concur in the National system."[20] He then added that he
thought the Convention was justified to go to any length in

recommending whatever was necessary to remedy the evils that had produced the Convention.

This speech was seized upon by Randolph and used to develop the first of two major arguments to legitimate the work of the Convention. "When the salvation of the Republic was at stake, it would be treason to our trust not to propose what we found necessary."[21] In a long and eloquent speech he undermined his opponents' arguments about the very limited nature of the calls for the Convention, arguing that it would have been indecent for any one state to list all the vices of the existing constitution without having the opinions of the others, and that at certain times ordinary cautions must be dispensed with. This is one of those occasions, he warned, and if the opportunity is not grasped, "after this experiment, the people will yield to despair."[22] Yates's version of this same speech contains several rhetorical flourishes that are absent in Madison's notes, namely, "It is said that power is wanting to institute such a government, but when our all is at stake, I will consent to any mode that will preserve us," and the epigram at the beginning of this chapter, "There are great seasons when persons with limited powers are justified in exceeding them, and a person would be contemptible not to risk it."[23]

So the first argument the Federalists made as to why they were not exceeding their mandate was an appeal from the *words* of the convention call to its *spirit*. Or as James Wilson put it, "The people expect relief from their present embarrassed situation, and look for it to this national convention."[24]

Hamilton makes the same argument two days later. "The States sent us here to provide for the exigencies of the Union. To rely on and propose any plan not adequate to these exigencies, merely because it was not clearly within our powers, would be to sacrifice the end to the means."[25]

It was a compelling argument and appears to have convinced a number of delegates. John Lansing tried to counter by saying the nub of the argument rested on a perception of public danger that he did not share, but by this time he was voicing a minority opinion.[26] Lansing had argued earlier that "New York would never have concurred in sending deputies . . . if she had supposed the deliberations were to turn on a consolidation of the States, and a National Government."[27] (Given the choices facing Governor Clinton, that's not necessarily so.)

The second pillar upon which the Federalists, led by Wilson, Madison, and Hamilton, built their case was that the Convention had only the power to *Recommend*; it needed no legal footing because it could take no legal steps. James Wilson "conceived himself authorized to *conclude nothing,* but . . . at liberty to *propose anything."*[28] (Italicized words were underscored by Madison when he revised his notes.) Hamilton felt no constraints for the same reason, "We can only propose and recommend—the power of ratifying or rejecting is still in the States."[29] Later, in *The Federalist Papers,* Madison was to claim with an air of innocence that the Convention was "merely advisory and recommendatory" and the Constitution it offered "of no more consequence than the paper on which it was written."[30] This time it was the Antifederalists who really had no answer.

In a sense the two arguments made in the convention, i.e., the public necessity for major changes in the structure of government, and that the changes were mere recommendations, and it was up to the states to accept or reject them, preempted the legality question during the ratification debates. One enraged Antifederalist summed up his frustrations in a letter worth quoting at length:

> They [the Convention] had no other authority to act in this manner than what was derived from their *commissions*—when they ceased to act *in conformity thereto* they ceased to be a federal convention and had no more *right* to propose to the United States the new form of government that an equal number of other gentlemen who might voluntarily have assembled for this purpose—the members of the Convention, therefore, having the merit of a work of supererogation, have thereby inferred no kind of obligation on the States to *consider,* much less to adopt *this plan of consolidation* of the Union! What a question is this to be *taken up* and *decided* by thirty-nine *gentlemen* who had no public [sic] authority whatever *for discussing it!*[31] [Emphasis in original.]

One can imagine Madison shrugging his shoulders and saying, "So?" Underlying the whole constitution-writing enterprise was an enormous gamble that if the people could see the new document and vote on it, that would provide all the legitimacy needed.

THE LEGITIMACY ARGUMENT DURING RATIFICATION

As the Convention went into its final days, the issue of legality was, for all practical purposes, settled, or, if one prefers, ignored. Instead, debate turned to strategies for getting the new constitution ratified. Delegates knew it was hopeless to give the document to Congress for its approbation. The unanimity requirement meant Rhode Island, which refused even to send delegates, could scuttle the whole enterprise. Instead, the delegates voted to set up a new procedure for approval: the draft would be forwarded to Congress, "that it should afterwards be submitted to a convention of delegates, chosen in each State by the people thereof, under the recommendation of its legislature, for their assent and ratification; and that each convention assenting to and ratifying the same should give notice thereof to the United States in Congress assembled."[32]

What the Founders did, in other words, was to send the document *through* the recognized governmental bodies, i.e., Congress and the state legislatures, to conventions in each state. It is remarkable that first Congress, then the legislatures of twelve states, did indeed forward the document, and in so doing, whether they intended to or not, added an aura of legitimacy. The question of the Convention's right to propose so radical a change was raised often and vigorously, but it was too late; as we see in the next chapter, attention had already turned to ways to amend the document, not reject it. Still, in *Federalist* No. 40, Madison felt compelled to provide one last defense for the Convention's actions. This is the most complete justification for the actions of the Convention that was made at the time and is reprinted in its entirety in Appendix II for the convenience of the readers. A summary is simply that:

[The delegates] must have reflected, that in all great changes of established governments, forms ought to give way to substance; that a rigid adherence in such cases to the former, would render nominal and negatory the transcendant and precious right of the people to "abolish or alter their governments as to them shall seem most likely to effect their safety and happiness," since it is impossible for the people spontaneously and universally to move in concert toward their object, and it is therefore essential that such changes be instituted by some *informal* and *unauthorized propositions*, made by some patriotic and respectable citizen or number of citizens.[33] [The words in quotation marks, Madison, in a not too subtle self-justification, took directly from the Declaration of Independence.]

So, did the first Constitutional Convention run away? Opponents could (and still do) answer with an emphatic yes! The Federalists' answer was an equally emphatic no, but it was a no given on another, more sophisticated level of discourse. They would readily grant that the Convention went beyond the limiting words of its call. As Gouverneur Morris proclaimed, "This Convention is unknown to the Confederation."[34] But they argued strenuously that they did what needed to be done; that, although they ignored the words, they remained faithful to the mandate of the convention call.

The Founders did not come to the Convention with a hidden agenda. They had publicly urged for years the need for a strong national government, nor, once assembled, did they suddenly veer off in reckless disregard of their stated purpose. They reflected and debated often on the propriety of proposing a radically new plan of government. Their ultimate defense, and one for which there is no answer, is that they only *proposed* a new plan of government. Opponents and members of the various elected governments had ample opportunity to debate and reject the constitution. They came close to doing so.

That new plan was accepted, however grudgingly, by Congress, by the state legislatures, and by state conventions. Acceptance was vindication and legitimation. This was in no sense a coup d'état or revolution. The Founders did not seize power first, then seek approval—always a dubious path to legitimacy. Instead they proposed an idea and sought acceptance before any changes were made in government. Did the Convention run away? Only in the sense that the nation itself ran away from a stifling, failing system in which it had "legally" trapped itself and embraced a new idea and a new system of government.

NOTES

1. Max Farrand, ed., *The Records of the Federal Convention of 1787* (New Haven: Yale University Press, 1966), I, p. 14.

2. Alexander Hamilton, *The Federalist Papers*, Jacob E. Cooke, ed. (Cleveland: Meridian Books, 1965), *Federalist* No. 22, p. 145.

3. "Vices of the Political System of the United States," April 1787 in Gaillard Hunt, ed., *The Writings of James Madison*, vol. II, pp. 361–369 (New York: G. P. Putnam's Sons, 1900–1910).

4. Richard S. Kay, "The Creation of Constitutions in Canada and the United States," *Canada–United States Law Journal* III, p. 125, 1984.

5. Farrand, *Records of the Convention*, III, p. 31.

6. See Andrew C. McLaughlin, *The Confederation and the Constitution, 1783–1789* (New York: Crowell-Collier, 1962).

7. Clinton Rossiter, *1787: The Grand Convention* (New York: Macmillan, 1966), pp. 49–50.

8. Madison letter of February 24, 1787 to Pendleton, in Rossiter, *1787*, p. 72.

9. September 14, 1786, in C. C. Tansill, ed., *Documents Illustrative of the Formation of the Union of American States*, House Doc. 398, 69th Congress, 1st Sess., 1927.

10. Records of the Continental Congress, p. 540ff.

11. The states were Virginia, New Jersey, New Hampshire, Pennsylvania, North Carolina, Delaware, and Georgia.

12. Letter to Edmund Randolph, February 18, 1787.

13. Letter to George Washington, February 11, 1787.

14. Rossiter, *1787*, p. 86.

15. Letter of Rufus King to Elbridge Gerry, February 18, 1787.

16. Kay, *"Creation of Constitutions,"* p. 126.

17. Specifically, Randolph began with four resolutions, the first of which was that the Articles ought to be "so corrected and enlarged as to accomplish the defects proposed by their institutions, namely, common defense, security of liberty and general welfare." Gouverneur Morris noted that this resolution was incompatible with the following three resolutions: (1) that a merely federal union would accomplish the objectives of the Articles of Confederation, (2) that treaties among sovereign states would not do it either, and (3) that a national government with an executive legislature and judiciary ought to be estab-

lished. After Morris made his observation, Randolph simply withdrew
his first resolution, but not the next three.

18. Farrand, *Records of the Convention,* I, p. 39.
19. Ibid., p. 178.
20. Ibid., p. 255.
21. Ibid.
22. Ibid., p. 256.
23. Ibid., p. 262.
24. Ibid., p. 261.
25. Ibid., p. 283.
26. Ibid., p. 336.
27. Ibid., p. 249.
28. Ibid., p. 253.
29. Ibid., p. 295.
30. *Federalist* No. 40, p. 264.
31. Letters of "A Republican Federalist" in C. Kenyon, ed., *The Antifederalist,* 1966, p. 114.
32. Resolution of the Convention, September 17, 1787, in Farrand,
Records of the Convention II, p. 665.
33. *Federalist* No. 40.
34. Farrand, *Records of the Convention* II, p. 92.

3

MADISON'S OPPOSITION TO A SECOND CONVENTION

JAMES MADISON IS commonly cited as an opponent of a second constitutional convention, especially by those late twentieth-century opponents of such a convention. The records refute this simplistic conclusion. Madison's opposition was not to conventions in general; rather, he opposed a specific plan to call a convention in 1788 before the national government was established, not the idea of a second convention if and when deficiencies were identified after experience with the new system of government. Although no friend of frequent conventions, Madison was prepared to use them, only for "great and extraordinary occasions."

In the recent debate over whether to call a constitutional convention to propose a balanced budget amendment, opponents were fond of quoting James Madison's letter to George Lee Turberville of November 2, 1788, stating his objection to a second convention. Indeed, Madison wrote with some eloquence:

If a General Convention were to take place for the avowed and sole purpose of revising the Constitution, it would naturally consider itself as having a greater latitude than the Congress appointed to administer and support as well as to amend the system; it would consequently give greater agitation to the public mind; and election into it would be courted by the most violent partizans [sic] on both sides; it would probably consist of the most heterogeneous characters; would be the very focus of that flame which had already too much heated men of all parties; would no doubt contain individuals of insidious views, who under the mask of seeking alterations popular in some parts but inadmissible in other parts of the Union might have a dangerous opportunity of sapping the very foundation of the fabric. Under all these circumstances it seems scarcely to be presumable that the deliberations of the body could be conducted in harmony, or terminate the general good. Having witnessed the difficulties and dangers experienced by the first Convention which assembled under every propitious circumstance, I should tremble for the result of a Second . . . [1]

Yet a review of the context in which he wrote indicates that translating his words into a supposed opposition to a convention in the 1990s is problematic, if not wholly unwarranted. The records of the founding period clearly indicate two facts: (1) Madison supported the convention mode of amendment as a matter of political principle, although he was concerned about the practicalities of calling a convention, and (2) his opposition to a second convention was opposition to a very specific, immediate plan to call a second convention *before* the national government was established, not to the concept of a second convention if and when deficiencies were found based on experience under the new system of government. We may consider each of these points in turn.

THE CONVENTION MODE OF AMENDMENT

In the Virginia Plan, which was drawn up prior to the opening of the federal convention and was the basis for initial discussion and debate, Resolution 13 proposed "that provision ought to be made for the amendment of the Articles of Union whensoever it shall seem necessary, and that the assent of the National Legislature ought not to be required thereto."[2] Introduced by Edmund Randolph on May 29, Resolution 13 was considered on June 5. Discussion zeroed in on the provision for excluding the legislature, not on whether the convention mode was appropriate. Charles Pinckney of South Carolina "doubted the propriety or necessity of it,"[3] i.e., excluding the

legislature from the amendment process, but he was countered
by Elbridge Gerry of Massachusetts, who not only emphasized
the need for periodic revision of the Constitution but defended
the states' ability to act responsibly: "Nothing had yet happened
in the States where this provision existed to prove its impro-
priety."[4] Apparently the issue was not yet clearly understood
and further discussion was postponed for a week.

In reporting the next consideration of the amendment procedure on June 11, Madison observed that "several members
did not see the necessity of the [Resolution] at all, nor the propriety of making the comment of the National Legislature unnecessary."[5] Colonel George Mason, a fellow Virginian, was
clearly not among the members Madison had in mind. He
staunchly defended both the need for an amendment provision
and the propriety of excluding the legislature:

The plan now to be formed will certainly be defective, as the Confederation has been found on trial to be. Amendments therefore will be
necessary and it will be better to provide for them, in an easy, regular
and Constitutional way than to trust to chance and violence. It would
be improper to require the consent of the National Legislature, because they may abuse their power, and refuse their consent on that
very account.[6]

Mason's eloquence won acceptance for the principle that an
amendment procedure was needed, but he was not able to persuade the delegates to exclude the legislature. This reluctance
is understandable on two counts. First, since the whole thrust
of the convention was to strengthen the national government,
members may have been reluctant to take what certainly appeared to be a step back toward state control. Second, at least
twenty-one of the thirty-nine delegates were sitting members of
the Confederate Congress—at that point the closest approxi-
mation there was to a national legislature—and may not have
taken kindly to any suggestion that they were not to be trusted.

In any event the matter was tabled again and in late July
given to a drafting committee rather quaintly called the Committee of Detail. This committee on August 6 proposed an
amendment procedure that included a role for the legislatures.

It read as follows: "On application of the Legislatures of two-thirds of the states in the Union, for an amendment of this Constitution, the Legislature of the United States shall call a convention for that purpose."[7] This amendment was adopted August 30, but not before Gouverneur Morris proposed "that the Legislatures should be left at liberty to call a Convention, whenever they please."[8] However, at that point he could garner no support and the article was adopted without amendment.

On September 10, Elbridge Gerry, a staunch republican who was becoming increasingly uneasy with the whole direction of the Convention,[9] moved to reconsider. He expressed his fears that "two-thirds of the States may obtain a Convention, a majority of which can bind the Union to innovations that may subvert the state constitutions altogether."[10] Gerry's motion received a second from an unexpected source—Alexander Hamilton. Indeed, Hamilton's fears were quite the opposite of Gerry's, i.e., he did not fear national power to subvert the states, but state power to subvert the nation. Also, whereas Gerry feared that amending would be too easy, Hamilton feared it would not be easy enough:

It was equally desirable now that an easy mode should be established for supplying defects which will probably appear in the new system. The mode proposed was not adequate. The State Legislatures will not apply for alteration but with a view to increase their own powers—the National Legislature will be the first to perceive and will be the most sensible to the necessity of amendments, and ought also to be empowered, whenever two-thirds of each branch should concur, to call a Convention . . . [11]

Madison at this point supported the call for reconsideration for yet a third reason, the vagueness of the terms, particularly the phrase "call a Convention for the Purpose . . ." How was a convention to be formed? By what rule decide? What would be the force of its act?[12] This is the first point at which those who claim Madison opposed the convention alternative would seem to find support. But the issue is not that clear. What Madison objected to was not the convention mode itself but the vagueness of the phraseology about how it would function. His questions, of course, were quite on point. In any event, granted the support of what might be called the political left (Gerry), right (Hamilton), and middle (Madison) in the Convention, the move to reconsider carried by a vote of nine to one, with one abstention.[13]

Discussion continued as delegates wrestled with ways to meet the various objections. Roger Sherman of Connecticut wanted to add the words: "Or the Legislature may propose amendments to the several states for their approbation but no amendment shall be binding until consented to by the several States." Sherman apparently meant that all the states would have to approve all amendments, a giant step backward from the Articles of Confederation provision. James Wilson of Pennsylvania quickly offered a motion to make consent of two-thirds of the states adequate. His motion narrowly lost by a vote of five to six. Wilson then proposed that three-fourths of the states approve amendment. This motion was accepted unanimously.

With that conflict resolved, Madison offered a substitute wording for the whole article:

The legislature of the United States whenever two-thirds of both Houses shall deem necessary, or on the application of two-thirds of the legislatures of the several States, shall propose amendments to this Constitution, which shall be valid for all intents and purposes as part thereof, when the same shall have been ratified by three-fourths at least of the Legislatures of the several States, or by Conventions in three-fourths thereof, as one or the other mode of ratification may be proposed by the legislature of the United States.[14]

Hamilton seconded the motion and it carried on a nine-to-one vote. The Madison-Hamilton substitution left out the convention mode of proposing amendments altogether, and the reasoning here is significant. First, Hamilton was not opposed to the convention mode, as his earlier speech indicated, but was concerned that the national legislature be given equal footing with the states to propose amendments; for him it was a balance-of-power issue.

Madison's reasons did not become clear until September 15,

the last day of formal debate in the whole Convention. The proposed article had been returned from the Committee of Style in the language of the Madison-Hamilton resolution. George Mason of Virginia, one of the members who would shortly refuse to sign the finished document, objected that both proposed modes of amendment relied too heavily on Congress. If Congress were to become oppressive, which Mason believed it would, the people would have no convenient way to propose amendments to rid themselves of the oppressive actions. He wanted at least one mode of amendment that did not involve Congress.[15] At that point Gouverneur Morris and Elbridge Gerry offered an amendment to require Congress to call a convention on application of two-thirds of the states.

Madison did not so much object to this motion as to comment that he did not think it was necessary. He "did not see why Congress would not be as much bound to propose amendments applied for by two-thirds of the States as to call a Convention on the like application."[16] He went on to add that he "saw no objection however against providing for a Convention for the purpose of amendments except only that difficulties might arise as to the form, the quorum, etc., which in Constitutional regulations ought to be as much as possible avoided."[17]

There we have it. Madison did *not* propose that the convention mode be inserted into the Constitution for two reasons: he thought it unnecessary and he thought there might be technical difficulties that required technical regulations of the type he thought ought to be avoided in writing a constitution. But neither did Madison oppose the convention mode of amendment. Indeed, when the Morris-Gerry proposal was voted on, it was passed unanimously, i.e., with Madison's support. In this regard Madison's attitude toward the convention mode of amendment was strikingly parallel to his attitude toward a Bill of Rights. He opposed including a Bill of Rights not because he was against civil liberties but because he thought such a bill unnecessary and that there were certain difficulties, i.e., the inclusion of some rights in such a bill might imply that others were not protected.[18] Nevertheless, when such a Bill of Rights was insisted upon, Madison was supportive. We can therefore conclude without a shadow of a doubt that Madison was not opposed to the convention mode of amendment in principle. Indeed the only real difference he saw between the two modes can be explained in terms of efficiency.

THE SECOND CONVENTION PROPOSAL

If Madison was not opposed to the convention mode in principle, there was one convention he vehemently opposed in practice. On August 31, in the midst of a discussion about how the new Constitution should be presented to the Confederate Congress and to the states, Colonel Mason dropped a bombshell. He announced that:

he would sooner chop off his right hand than put it to the Constitution as it now stands. He wished to see some points not yet decided brought to a decision, before being compelled to give a final opinion on this article. Should these points be improperly settled, his wish would then be to bring the whole subject before another general Convention.[19]

Both Gouverneur Morris and Edmund Randolph jumped at the suggestion, but for quite different reasons. Morris stated that he had long wanted a second convention that would have the firmness to provide a vigorous government, something the first was afraid to do. Randolph thought that if the final draft were such that he could sign it, the state conventions should be free to propose amendments to a second general convention, which could either accept or reject them.

The matter was dropped for the moment, but on September 10, Randolph brought the subject up twice. The first time he merely complained that he had recognized the need for radical changes and so had brought forward a set of republican principles as the basis for reform. However, they had been so altered in the course of the Convention that now he thought state conventions should consider the plan and offer amendments, which would then be considered at a second general convention.[20]

Some time later in the debate, he raised the issue again on a much more personal level, claiming he would not sign the document unless such a provision were included. This time he apparently got the Convention's attention. Benjamin Franklin seconded his motion to call for a second convention, but Mason, in a conciliatory move, requested that the motion be tabled for a few days to see whether steps could be taken to address Randolph's objections.[21]

Apparently not enough could be accomplished, for on the final full working day of the Convention, Randolph made a last dramatic motion. Even though he was pained and embarrassed to be differing from the majority there, he felt the powers given to Congress so dangerous that the whole plan should be given to state conventions for amendments, and then the results turned over to another general convention.[22] Randolph followed his motion by stating that he would refuse to sign the document and might even oppose it in Virginia if his motion were defeated. This time Colonel Mason did nothing to modify his friend's stand. Quite the opposite. Not only did he second Randolph's motion, but he added another compelling argument for the second convention:

This Constitution had been formed without the knowledge or idea of the people. A second Convention will know more of the sense of the people, and be able to provide a system more consonant to it. It is improper to say to the people, take this or nothing. As the Constitution now stands, he could neither give it his support or vote in Virginia; and he could not sign here what he could not support there. With the expedient of another Convention as proposed, he could sign.[23]

This was political pressure indeed, coming as it did from two of the workhorses of the Convention. But the delegates had learned too much during the past months to be swayed. Charles Pinckney of South Carolina, evincing some respect for the opinions just stated, nevertheless warned of the consequences of getting amendments from each state:

Nothing but confusion and contrariety could spring from the experiment. The States will never agree in their plans—And the Deputies to a second Convention coming together under the discordant impressions of their Constituents, will never agree. Conventions are serious things, and ought not to be repeated. He was not without objections as well as others to the plan. . . . But apprehending the danger of a general confusion, and an ultimate decision by the Sword, he should give the plan his support.[24]

Elbridge Gerry, who turned out to be the third nonsigner, rose to make one last pitch. After spelling out eight minor and three major deficiencies of the Constitution, he concluded, "Under such a view of the Constitution, the best that could be done . . . was to provide for a second general convention."[25] The effort was in vain. When the question was put on Randolph's motion, the state delegations unanimously rejected the call for a second convention.

What was transpiring here was not an isolated attempt by three disgruntled delegates to force changes in the document, but one episode in a long battle between two overlapping, but increasingly distinct groups, Federalists and Antifederalists, to define and structure the very nature of American government for future generations.[26] The Antifederalists had been bested both in the call for the Constitutional Convention and in the form of the Constitution written there. In the call for a second convention they had hit upon a scheme to recoup their losses. Agreement to call a second convention to consider a specific document, the just-completed Constitution, and specific amendments as proposed by the states, would give them an unprecedented opportunity to organize, frame strategies, and campaign for what they were certain the majority of American citizens wanted, a truly republican form of government.

The call for a second convention did have a certain intellectual appeal, and even a number of Federalists wavered.[27] If the Federalists did, as they claimed, speak for the "weight of the community," why should they fear a chance for the community to affirm and even suggest changes in the document they had just drafted? Mason had a valid point, after all. The document had been forged in secret, and a take-it-or-leave-it approach could hardly be seen as fair, to say nothing of being republican in nature, especially when a golden opportunity arose to determine the sense of the community before formally establishing the new form of government, i.e., through a second convention.

The Federalists in the Convention, however, could not be seduced by the siren songs of republican principle and intellectual consistency. Having lived through the near-collapse of the Convention over the issue of representation and knowing they had barely been able to build bridges just above the torrents of irreconcilable state interests, they realized they could not afford to open the floodgates to another surge of state demands. Madison had not spoken against a second convention during the first one, preferring to let Pinckney advocate the Federalist position. But he knew the battle was not over; it had merely been postponed and would arise again in the ratification struggle.

RATIFICATION BATTLES

Despite the refusal of three prominent members to sign the document, or even acquiesce in a maneuver to make it *look* like there had been unanimity, the Convention adjourned on a note of euphoria, tempered by the realization that the battle for ratification was still ahead. Whereas most of the weary delegates headed home, Madison and other delegates who were also elected members of the Confederate Congress left immediately for New York to "receive" their handiwork officially and shepherd it through a potentially hostile Congress, which, after all, was being asked to sign its own death warrant. Even at this late date, however, congressional opponents lacked the will to resist, and the proposed Constitution was forwarded to the states. In the ensuing struggle, Madison had to deal directly with the question of a second convention on three occasions: during ratification battles in the states, particularly in New York and Virginia; during his own campaign for election to the House, and in the first Congress. We may look at each briefly.

Ratification in the States

The first votes for ratification came easily. Delaware, New Jersey, and Connecticut affirmed their allegiance because Federalists were firmly in control in these states and their citizens believed they would be protected from their larger, predatory neighbors in ways they never were under the Articles. Georgia ratified because it desperately needed outside help to ward off the Creek Indians, and Pennsylvania followed because Federalists there rammed the call for a ratifying convention through the legislature and then conducted elections so quickly that they achieved a 46–25 advantage in delegates.[28] The rest did not come so easily.

The Antifederalists lacked both a coherent alternative plan to the Constitution and a national organization. Their struggle against ratification was waged in thirteen different arenas and for the most part by local partisans. Federalists, in contrast, had several factors in their favor. Not only did they have a plan, but they also had the backing of the only two truly national heroes, Washington and Franklin. Moreover, they were able to hammer away on three ideas their opponents could never quite refute:

(1) Only those men who had been in the Convention could understand the difficulties of writing a legitimate charter for a "numerous and varied people"; (2) in the light of these difficulties, the Convention had produced the best of all possible charters and there was "no prospect of getting a better"; (3) rejection of this charter, or even a lengthy delay in ratifying it would mean disunion, disorder and finally, disaster for the United States.[29]

What the Antifederalists did have behind them, and a point too often forgotten, was a majority of the population. This was admittedly something of a "silent majority" made up of the suspicious, the openly hostile, the uncommitted, and a large mass of the apathetic.[30] But it did exist, and there was a real potential that it could be mobilized. Nor was leadership absent. Indeed, Madison expressed surprise that so many respectable, established leaders throughout the states actively opposed the Constitution.[31]

Federalists had first to confront the problem of the Antifederalist majority in Massachusetts. When the state convention gathered on January 9, 1788, an informal survey revealed a small majority to be opponents of the Constitution. Not only did the Federalists engage in hard, behind-the-scenes politicking, but they hit upon a strategy that turned out to be a key to success in the ratification drive. The strategy was twofold: (1) they listened respectfully to the Antifederalist leaders, and when they responded, often brilliantly, they tended to do so in a conciliatory manner; then (2) they promised to make recommendations for amendments to be considered by the first Congress. Both steps were critical. Antifederalists pushed for *conditional* ratification, the condition being a second convention to consider the amendments. On this issue the Federalists bent but never broke. They promised to *recommend* amendments, but refused to accept amendments as a condition for ratification. This tactic made it possible to overcome the Antifederalist majority, and with one exception it was quickly picked up in other states.[32] Massachusetts ratified on February 6, 1788, with a 187–168 majority.

The New Hampshire Convention, meeting on February 13, ended any euphoria the Federalists might have felt after their victory in Massachusetts. A substantial majority of the 104 delegates came instructed to vote against the Constitution. The Federalists barely managed to engineer a postponement of the convention until June. By that time, news of the Massachusetts and Maryland ratifications had filtered out to the hinterlands, and strenuous politicking by the Federalists, accompanied by agreement to recommend amendments, changed enough minds to produce a 57-47 vote for ratification. The New Hampshire convention proposed twelve amendments to accompany its approval of the Constitution, three more than South Carolina, which had given its approval during New Hampshire's recess.

Before New Hampshire's vote was known, Virginia was deep in the throes of a battle between political titans. Believing his state to have the crucial ninth vote, Patrick Henry was determined to force a second convention at all costs. He was convinced that Virginia could get a much more powerful position and much stronger safeguards of its liberties through another convention. Supported by stalwarts such as George Mason, Richard Henry Lee, James Monroe, and others, Henry waged a fierce battle of words.[33] But Henry and his colleagues were met point-counterpoint by Madison, who took the high road of vision and principle, and punch-counterpunch by "Light Horse Harry" Lee, who took the low road of invective. For four weeks the debates raged, with delegate sympathies surging from side to side. But the Massachusetts strategy paid off. The Federalists accepted recommendation after recommendation for amendments, but no conditions, and when the final vote was tallied on June 25, ratification carried 89–79.[34]

The struggle in New York, just as critical, was if anything even more precarious. Fewer than 30 percent of the sixty-five convention delegates were committed Federalists, although a number of others were uncommitted. Ratification was helped immeasurably by the news that New Hampshire and Virginia had agreed, but what probably had the greatest influence was the threat that the southern counties, including New York City, might secede if New York State did not ratify. The Antifederalists, led by Governor Clinton, fought desperately against ratification without amendments. For all practical purposes, the New York convention was in a stalemate. Clinton's backers could muster enough votes to prevent unconditional ratification, but not enough to reject the Constitution outright. So a series of compromises was offered.

At one point Melancton Smith moved for unconditional ratification with the "reservation" that New York had the right to secede if the amendments proposed by the state were not acted on within six years. Hamilton objected so strongly that Smith withdrew his motion, but the next day it was reintroduced by John Lansing. Hamilton, fearing he could get no more, wavered, and wrote to Madison for his opinion. Madison was adamant: "Such conditional ratification would not make New York a member of the Union. The Constitution requires an adoption *in toto* and forever."[35] The Federalists stood fast, but a final and successful compromise almost proved their undoing. The compromise had been a unanimous concurrence in a resolution calling for a second convention to be sent to all the legislatures. The vote came on July 26 by a scant 30–27 margin, and was accompanied "by sixteen passionately declared rights, seven 'impressions,' four 'reservations,' thirty-two amendments and a circular letter to 'our sister states' calling for a second general convention."[36]

The battle for ratification in New York had led Madison, Hamilton, and Jay to write the now-classic *Federalist Papers*.[37] In

Federalist No. 49 Madison wrestles with a key ratification issue, how to prevent the national legislature from becoming tyrannical, and raises the convention issue somewhat obliquely. He expands on his classic argument that the size and divisions of the nation are its best protection, but along the way he disposes of alternative solutions. In this case, he analyzes Jefferson's proposal in *Notes on the State of Virginia* that "whenever any two of the three branches of government shall concur . . . that a convention is necessary for altering the Constitution, or correcting breaches of it, *a convention shall be called for the purpose.*"[38]

Madison's several objections to Jefferson's proposal shed some light on his attitude toward a second constitutional convention. First, the remedy will not reach to the problem of maintaining the equilibrium of government because it does not touch the potential problem of two branches acting in collusion against the third, and it does not prevent the legislature, the most likely source of tyranny, from using its contacts and popularity with the people to gain seats in the convention and thereby prevent the passage of any remedies to its tyranny.

Second, although acknowledging that a constitutional means ought to be provided for the people acting in their sovereign capacity to make fundamental decisions about their government, Madison feared that "*frequent* appeals would, in great measure, deprive the government of that veneration which time bestows on everything, and without which perhaps the wisest and freest governments would not possess the requisite stability."[39] Frequent resort to conventions has two problems. It does not allow for the development among citizens of the habits of attachment, loyalty, and trust, which lead to a reverence for law, and it tends to disturb public tranquillity by appeals to the passions and not the reason of the citizenry. The appeal would be to the passions because the public decision would be influenced by preexisting parties, parties springing out of the question itself, and as a result of the influences of distinguished community leaders attempting to sway public opinion. Madison concludes, "It is the reason alone of the public that ought to control and regulate the government. The passions ought to be controlled and regulated by the government."[40]

Madison's objections are to frequent conventions in which members of Congress would likely sit. What would he have thought of infrequent conventions from which members of Congress would be excluded?[41] Although any answer must be speculative, *Federalist* No. 49 does give some clues. One finds a very cautious, wary Founder, but not one opposed to conventions in the proper circumstances, for as he remarks about the Jefferson proposal, "There is certainly great force in this reasoning, and it must be allowed to prove that a constitutional road to the decision of the people ought to be marked out and kept open, for certain great and extraordinary occasions."[42] In any event, and whatever the impact of the *Federalist Papers,* with New York in, a major battle was won. North Carolina and Rhode Island eventually saw their ways to joining the Union, but Madison's struggles over a second convention were not yet over.[43] The circular letter turned out to have a brief but mischievous history.

Battle for Election

Both Madison and Patrick Henry saw the New York circular letter for what it was: a late, but potent tool to rally opponents of the Constitution for yet another battle. Madison wrote to a friend, "If an *early* convention cannot be parried, it is seriously to be feared that the system which has resisted so many direct attacks may be at last undermined by its enemies."[44] Indeed, even Washington had trepidations, as a letter to Benjamin Lincoln in late August 1788 indicates: "I apprehend that the New York circular is intended to bring on a general convention *at too early a period,* and by referring the subject to the legislatures *to set everything afloat again.*"[45]

Meanwhile, Patrick Henry was active again. He had been devastated by the vote in the Virginia convention but, remarkably enough, not deterred. After the vote, his last words to the convention had been, "My head, my hand and my heart shall be at liberty to remove the defects of the system in a constitutional way."[46] The New York circular letter was just the boost he needed to continue the struggle. Henry's strategy was twofold: have the state legislatures, or Congress itself if the legis-

latures failed, call a convention, then work for the election of
Antifederalists to the new Congress. But it was not to be. Despite Henry's efforts, only four states were willing to call for a
convention: Virginia, New York, North Carolina, and Rhode
Island. Among the others convention ardor had cooled. The
state legislatures had accepted the decisions of their ratifying
conventions and were busy creating congressional districts and
appointing Senators.[47]

After Henry succeeded in getting a convention call through
the Virginia assembly, he focused his energies on the selection
of senators and congressmen. A top priority was to deny his
nemesis, Madison, a place in either chamber. Despite the Federalist victory in the ratifying convention, Henry was able to
prevail upon the legislature to appoint two Antifederalists,
Richard Henry Lee and William Grayson, as senators. Henry
seemingly stopped at nothing. He is reported at one point to
have threatened darkly that Madison's election would "terminate in producing rivulets of blood throughout the land."[48] Next
he arranged to gerrymander a congressional district to include
Madison's own Orange County with seven counties considered
to be Antifederalist strongholds. Apparently a rumor campaign
was started as well, aimed at the large number of Baptist voters,
that Madison's enthusiasm for religious liberty had waned and
that he was unwilling to add amendments to protect the rights
of conscience.[49] Henry also prevailed upon James Monroe, a
well-known, popular, and noncontroversial figure, to oppose
Madison.

Madison, however, was not so easily done in. At the frantic
urging of his friends, he rushed to Virginia to campaign, a task
he wholeheartedly detested. Two factors worked in his favor.
First was a series of open discussions (they could hardly be called
debates) with the genial Monroe, which seemed to reassure the
citizens that Madison was no foe of personal liberties. Second
was a series of letters to followers, strategically made public,
which explained Madison's opposition to a second convention
and his willingness to add amendments that, in his judgment,
would not endanger the republic. It was in the midst of this
campaign that his letter to Turberville was written.[50] Unfortunately this letter is rarely quoted in its entirety, nor is Madison's

letter to George Eve, a Baptist preacher, in which the Founder summarizes his views on a second convention quite concisely.[51] In the letter to Turberville Madison laid out four objections to a second convention. Each was related to the specific circumstances of 1788–1789, although instructive for later times as well. First, a convention would:

add to the difference among the States on the merits [of Amendments] another and an unnecessary difference concerning the mode. There are amendments which in themselves will probably be agreed to by all the States, and pretty certainly by the requisite proportion of them. If they be contended for in the mode of a Convention, there are unquestionably a number of States who will be so averse and apprehensive as to the mode, that they will reject the merits rather than agree to the mode. A convention therefore does not appear to be the most convenient or probable channel for getting to the object.[52]

Madison's second objection was simply that calling a convention was inefficient and time-consuming. Congress could do in a day, with the same result, what would otherwise require action by two-thirds of the states. The third objection, quoted at the beginning of this chapter, makes the point that safety for the republic from undue public agitation is important. The last sentence of Madison's statement is rarely quoted in its entirety, yet it is instructive: "Having witnessed the difficulties and dangers experienced by the First Convention, which assembled under every propitious circumstance, I should tremble for the result of a Second, *meeting in the present temper of America and under all the disadvantages I have mentioned.*"[53] It seems quite clear that Madison's worry about the safety of another convention was tied to the uncertain loyalties and bitter divisions that followed the ratification struggles.

Finally, Madison opposed a second convention because he feared it would be misunderstood in Europe, that it would be seen as a "dark and threatening cloud hanging over the Constitution just established," and would undermine the seeds of liberty that had been sown, particularly in France. Madison pointedly ended his letter with reference to a loan from the Dutch government, which had been given with the understanding that the new Constitution would be "certainly, speedily, quietly and finally established."

As Madison's letters make clear, his opposition to a second convention was both broader and narrower than present-day commentators realize. It was broader in that he saw it as an uncertain mode, inefficient, risky, and creating an unfavorable impression in Europe, and narrower in that he was not opposed to another convention in general if needed to improve the system. He was only opposed to a specific call for a general convention to be held before the new Constitution had been properly tested.

Madison's campaign for election to the House of Representatives was successful, and the final battle over the method for proposing amendments awaited his arrival in the new legislature.

Battle in the Congress

By the time Congress was organized and began functioning in May 1789, even Patrick Henry must have sensed the failure of his scheme for a second general convention. Before the Virginia call for a convention could be brought up, Madison requested that Congress itself propose a series of amendments to be sent to the states. On June 8, 1789, he presented twelve amendments from the lists requested by the states, ten of which compose the present Bill of Rights.[54] At that point the move for a second convention collapsed entirely.

After a review of the historical record, it seems clear that Madison's opposition was not to conventions in general but to a specific call for a second general convention before the nation had a chance to function under the Constitution and experience its strengths and weaknesses. He understood clearly that the convention proposed by Patrick Henry and other Antifederalists was not an attempt to fine-tune a fundamentally sound system, but an effort to renegotiate the fundamental compromises that had made a national charter possible in the first place. What Madison understood, and Henry did not, was the fragility of the compromises and the fundamental incompatibility of many of the Antifederalist demands with the nationalist objectives of the new Constitution.

It cannot be concluded, however, that because Madison fought so valiantly against a second convention in 1788 that he would be opposed to a convention called for a limited purpose today. The intervening years have provided precisely what Madison found lacking in 1788: (1) a time of trial to determine what would work and what would not under the Constitution, (2) a tradition of loyalty and commitment to constitutional values among the citizenry, and (3) stable mechanism, such as voting laws and bills for establishing the rules and procedures of a convention, by which to elect responsible delegates and resolve the technical difficulties of calling and conducting a convention.

Neither, on the other hand, can one enlist Madison's enthusiastic support for such a convention. He feared that if conventions were called with any frequency they could undermine development of a spirit of attachment among the citizens; he thought allowing members of Congress to run for convention seats would limit the effectiveness of a convention; and he worried about the technicalities of calling and conducting a convention. Ever the astute statesman and politician, Madison undoubtedly would have looked for the most effective means to resolve the conflicts inherent in a democratic society. Most certainly he would have saved the convention option for "great and extraordinary occasions."

NOTES

1. Robert A. Rutland and Charles F. Hobson, eds., *The Papers of James Madison,* Vol. 11 (Charlottesville: University Press of Virginia, 1977), pp. 330–332.

2. U.S. Constitutional Convention, 1787, *The Records of the Federal Convention of 1787,* Max Farrand, ed. (New Haven: Yale University Press, 1911), p. 22.

3. Ibid., pp. 121–122.

4. Ibid., p. 122. Gerry was referring here to the fact that several states already had provisions for amending their constitutions. Delaware, Maryland, and South Carolina made provisions for amendments to be initiated by their legislatures. Georgia, Massachusetts, New

Hampshire, Pennsylvania, and Vermont provided for amendments by convention.

5. Farrand, I, pp. 202–203.

6. Ibid.

7. Farrand, II, p. 188. Those who would see in this inclusion of the legislature the hand of Madison have to contend with the fact that he was not a member of the Committee of Detail. It was chaired by John Randolph of South Carolina. Other members were Edmund Randolph (VA), James Wilson (PA), Oliver Ellsworth (CT), and Nathaniel Gorham (MA).

8. Ibid., p. 468.

9. See Clinton Rossiter, *1787: The Grand Convention* (New York: Macmillan, 1966), p. 182.

10. Farrand, II, pp. 557–558.

11. Ibid.

12. Ibid.

13. New Jersey voted to retain the August 30 wording; New Hampshire was divided. Rhode Island, of course, had never sent delegates. Since two of the three New York delegates had already left, New York did not vote.

14. Farrand, II, p. 559.

15. Ibid., p. 629.

16. Ibid., pp. 629–630.

17. Ibid. The argument that Madison was not opposed to the convention mode in principle is strengthened by another exchange that occurred on August 31. Gouverneur Morris moved to strike out the convention means of ratification, "Leaving the States to pursue their own modes of ratifications." Madison responded at some length:

. . . [He] *considered it best to require Conventions.* Among other reasons, for this, that the powers given to the General Government being taken from the State Governments the Legislatures would be more disinclined than conventions composed in part at least of other men; and if disinclined, they could devise modes apparently promoting, but really thwarting the ratification. . . . The people were in fact, the fountain of all power and by resorting to them, all difficulties were got over. They could alter constitutions as they pleased. It was a principle in the Bill of Rights, that first principles might be resorted to. [Ibid., p. 476, emphasis added.]

Granted the conventions at issue were state ratifying conventions, not a national one, Madison here acknowledges two important points: (1) legislatures could be self-serving and devious, and (2) people do indeed have a right to, and should have the means to, overcome the resistance of self-serving legislatures.

18. Letter to Thomas Jefferson, October 17, 1788, in Gaylor Hunt, ed., *Writings of James Madison* (New York: G. P. Putnam's Sons, 1904), pp. 269, 271–174; also I *Annals of Congress* (1834), pp. 436–444. For Jefferson's perspective, see Bowers, "Jefferson and the Bill of Rights," *Virginia Law Review* 41 (1955), pp. 709, 712–714.

19. Farrand, II, p. 479.

20. Ibid., pp. 560–561.

21. Ibid., p. 564.

22. Ibid., p. 631.

23. Ibid., p. 632.

24. Ibid. One modern commentator has observed, "The reason for his [Pickney's] confusion is instructive. *His reason was that a second convention would be unable to produce agreement.* This is a very different concern from that of present opponents of a second constitutional convention, who fear precisely that a new convention *would* produce agreement. Jeffrey T. Bergner, "A Second Constitutional Convention: The View from the First Convention," *Hearing before the Subcommittee on the Constitution of the Committee on the Judiciary, United States Senate, Ninety-Sixth Congress,* p. 347.

25. Ibid., p. 633.

26. This point is convincingly argued by the late Herbert Storing in his introduction to *The Anti-Federalist: Writings by the Opponents of the Constitution* (Chicago: University of Chicago Press, 1986), pp. 2–4.

27. See letter from George Turberville to Madison, October 24, 1788. Compare to Turberville's letter of October 27, 1788, which triggered Madison's letter of November 2. See Rutland and Hobson, *Papers of Thomas Jefferson,* pp. 316–332.

28. It is instructive that so high-handed were the Federalists that opposition hardened, and despite three weeks of often brilliant debate, not a single vote was changed.

29. Rossiter, *1787*, p. 241.

30. There were, of course, no polls in 1787 to measure the extent of the opposition. One need not accept the overall thesis of Charles Beard's *An Economic Interpretation of the Constitution* (New York: Macmillan, 1935), or of Michael Parenti's "The Constitution as an Elitist Document," in *How Democratic Is the Constitution?* Robert A Goldwin and William A. Schambra, eds. (Washington, DC: American Enterprise Institute, 1980) to recognize that committed Federalists were a distinct minority at the beginning of the ratification process. Indeed the whole point of the ratification story is the winning over of the suspicious and the uncommitted. For one poignant example, see Rich-

ard B. Morris, *Witnesses at the Creation* (New York: New American Library, 1985), pp. 224–252.

31. Letter to Archibald Stuart, October 30, 1787, in *Writings of Madison*, V, 47.

32. The exception was Maryland. Here the Federalists had a solid majority. Rather than repeat the bitter Pennsylvania experience, the Federalists let their opponents, led by Samuel Chase and Luther Martin, speak as long as they desired, and never answered! After four days the opponents sank back exhausted, a vote was taken, and Maryland ratified by a vote of 63–11. Jonathan Elliot, ed., *The Debates of the State Conventions on the Adoption of the Federal Constitution*, as Recommended by the General Convention at Philadelphia in 1787 (Philadelphia, 1866), 2nd ed., II, pp. 547–556.

33. History has not been kind to Patrick Henry on this issue, but his foresight was far keener than that of many of his contemporaries, including Madison. Henry's fears focused on two developments he saw as inevitable under the proposed constitutional scheme: (1) power would inevitably flow away from the states into the national government, and (2) within the national government power would shift from the legislature to the presidency. Today we must admit he was right on both counts.

34. Without doubt George Washington's support was the single most important factor in the Virginia delegates' vote for ratification, but it alone was not enough; it took enormous effort by Madison to withstand Henry's persuasive rhetoric.

35. *Hamilton's Works*, I, p. 465.

36. Rossiter, *1787*, p. 253.

37. Clinton Rossiter, ed., *The Federalist Papers* (New York: New American Library, 1961).

38. *Federalist* No. 49, p. 313 (emphasis added).

39. Ibid., p. 314 (emphasis added).

40. Ibid., p. 317.

41. All present proposals for establishing the rules of a convention explicitly prohibit members of Congress from sitting in the convention.

42. *Federalist* No. 49, p. 314.

43. In fact, North Carolina and Rhode Island were the only states to insist on a second convention and the addition of amendments before they would ratify the Constitution. But with the ratification of New York, their ploy failed. *Elliot's Debates*, IV, 242. See Edward P. Smith, "The Movement Toward a Second Constitutional Convention in 1788," in *Essays in the Constitutional History of the United States in the*

Formative Period 1775–1789, J. Franklin Jameson, ed. (Boston: Hough-ton Mifflin, 1889), pp. 97, 108.

44. Rive's *Madison,* ii, p. 629 (emphasis added). (Quoted in Edward P. Smith, "The Movement Toward a Second Constitutional Conven-tion," p. 95)

45. Ibid., p. 630, (emphasis added). It is important to include these two letters as they clearly indicate that both Washington and Madison feared only an early convention called before the nation had a chance to begin functioning under the first constitution. This point is made even more clearly in a letter from Madison to Edmund Pendleton of October 20, 1788. "An *early* Convention threatens discord and mis-chief. It will be composed of the most heterogeneous characters—will be actuated by the party spirit reigning among their constituents—will comprehend men having insidious designs agst. [sic] the Union—and can scarcely therefore terminate in harmony or the public good. *Let the enemies to the System wait until some experience shall have taken place, and the business will be conducted with more light as well as with less heat"* (emphasis added).

46. Elliot's *Debates,* III, 652.

47. The reasoning given by the Pennsylvania House expressed the sentiments well: "The House does not perceive this Constitution want-ing in any of those fundamental principles which are calculated to ensure the liberties of their country. The happiness of America and the harmony of the Union depend upon suffering it to proceed un-disturbed in its operation by premature amendments. The House can-not, consistently with their duty to the good people of this state, or with affection to the citizens of the United States at large, concur with Virginia in their application to Congress for a convention of the states." *Pennsylvania Archives,* xi, p. 557.

48. Letter of Henry Lee to James Madison, November 19, 1788. In *Writings of James Madison.*

49. This is not without irony, since Madison's classic *Memorial and Remonstrance* had been written in 1785 precisely to oppose a proposed tax to support religious education. The tax had been urged by none other than Patrick Henry.

50. Rutland and Hobson, *Papers of James Madison,* pp. 330–332.

51. Letter to George Eve, January 2, 1789. "I have intimated that the amendments ought to be proposed by the first Congress. I prefer this mode to that of a General Convention, 1st. because it is the ex-peditious mode. A convention must be delayed, until 2/3 of the State Legislatures shall have applied for one; and afterwards the amend-ments must be submitted to the States; whereas if the business be un-

dertaken by Congress the amendments may be prepared and submitted in March next. 2dly. because it is the most certain mode. There are not a few States who will absolutely reject the proposal of a Convention, and yet not be averse to amendments in the other mode. Lastly, it is the safest mode. The Congress, who will be appointed to execute as well as to amend the Government, will probably be careful not to destroy or endanger it. A convention, on the other hand, meeting in the present ferment of parties, and containing perhaps insidious characters from different parts of America, would at least spread a general alarm, and be but too likely to turn everything into confusion and uncertainty."

52. Letter to George Turberville, November 2, 1788.

52. Ibid. (emphasis added).

54. Two amendments, dealing with the scale of representation in the House and congressional compensation, did not get the requisite approval of three-fourths of the states.

4

The History of Attempts to Call a Constitutional Convention

In his classic treatise *Congressional Government,* written in 1885, Woodrow Wilson described the United States Constitution's provisions for amendment as "the cumbrous machinery in Article V."[1] At the time Wilson penned his description of the Constitution's amendment process, only fifteen amendments had been added to the original document. (The first ten additions were adopted as the Bill of Rights in 1791). In the century since Wilson's book was published, just eleven more articles have been appended to the Constitution. With one exception, all twenty-six amendments have resulted from the procedure outlined in the first provision of Article V, namely, initiation by two-thirds majority of both houses of Congress with subsequent ratification by the legislatures of three-fourths of the states. Congress deviated from this procedure only once, in 1933 when it submitted the Twenty-first Amendment repealing Prohibition (Amendment Eighteen) to state conventions rather than to state legislatures for ratification.[2]

Undoubtedly, the most "cumbrous machinery" in Article V has been the amendment by convention provision. To date more than 400 applications calling for a convention to propose constitutional amendments have been presented to Congress by state legislatures. Yet no convention call has garnered the necessary

two-thirds majority of states required to force Congress to convene a meeting to propose amendments.[3]

The more than 400 petitions to Congress requesting a constitutional convention have included supplications from all fifty
states. The proliferation of applications for constitutional conventions is distinctly a phenomenon of America's second century. More than 90 percent have reached Congress in the twentieth century, and approximately 50 percent have come since
the 1960s.[4]

THE FIRST CENTURY: GENERAL CONVENTION CALLS

In the first hundred years after the country's founding, only
ten applications for a constitutional convention were submitted
by states to the Congress. Nevertheless, though few in number,
they addressed three significant constitutional crises in the nation's first century.

The initial two petitions grew out of the founding era itself.
As discussed in Chapter 3, even before the Philadelphia convention had adjourned in 1787, delegates had begun requesting a second meeting to address inadequacies perceived in the
original document.[5] Opponents of the Constitution particularly
feared the lack of a bill of rights and voiced their reservations
in the state ratifying conventions. Despite the opposition
mounted by these Antifederalists, the required number of nine
states had ratified the new Constitution by June 1788—just nine
months after the submission of the document to the states.[6]

Yet Virginia and New York had still not adopted the Constitution and attention turned to their contentious ratification
conventions. Without the support of two of the country's largest states, the new Union had little hope of success. After long
and bitter debates, Virginia became the tenth state to ratify on
June 25, 1788, with a declaration "that whatsoever imperfec-
tions may exist in the constitution ought rather to be examined
in the mode prescribed therein than to bring the Union into
danger by a delay with a hope of obtaining Amendments previous to the Ratification." The Virginia document of ratification

also included a recommended bill of rights for the first Congress' consideration.[7]

One month after Virginia's adoption of the Constitution, New York followed suit but with a conditional ratification that included an ominous letter to be circulated to the states calling for a second constitutional convention.[8] New York Governor George Clinton, a staunch Antifederalist and president of the New York ratifying convention, signed the letter, drafted by the convention delegates, which renewed doubts over the omission of a bill of rights. The New York letter urged the state legislatures to petition Congress for a general convention to rectify the problem.[9]

The letter received a supportive welcome from Virginia's legislature, which was dominated by Antifederalists. A minority of Virginia legislators argued that a petition to Congress should allow a choice between congressional proposal of amendments or the calling of a convention to propose them. Such alternatives would have allowed Congress to choose the less disruptive means of amending the new Constitution. Nonetheless, the majority in the Virginia legislature voted to petition Congress to call a convention.[10] Virginia's action, taken on November 14, 1788, and recorded by the House of Representatives on May 6, 1789,[11] represented the first formal state application to Congress for a constitutional convention.

The heart of the Virginia application read as follows:

In making known to you the objections of the people of this Commonwealth to the new plan of Government, we deem it unnecessary to enter into a particular detail of its defects, which they consider as involving all the great and unalienable rights of freemen. For their sense on this subject we beg leave to refer you to the proceedings of their late convention, and the sense of the House of Delegates, as expressed in their resolutions of the 30th day of October, 1788.

We think proper, however, to declare that, in our opinion, as those objections were not founded in speculative theory, but deduced from principles which have been established by the melancholy example of other nations in different ages, so they will never be removed until the cause itself shall cease to exist. The sooner, therefore, the public apprehensions are quieted, and the Government is possessed of the confidence of the people, the more salutary will be its operations and the longer its duration.

The cause of amendments we consider as a common cause; and, since concessions have been made from political motives which we conceive may endanger the republic, we trust that a commendable zeal will be shown for obtaining those provisions which experience has taught us are necessary to secure from danger the unalienable rights of human nature.

The anxiety with which our countrymen press for the accomplishment of this important end will ill admit of delay. The slow forms of Congressional discussion and recommendation, if indeed they should ever agree to any change, would, we fear, be less certain of success. Happily for their wishes, the constitution has presented an alternative, by admitting the submission to a convention of the States. To this, therefore, we resort, as the source from whence they are to derive relief from their present apprehensions.

We do, therefore, in behalf of our constituents, in the most earnest and solemn manner, make this application to Congress, that a convention be immediately called, of deputies from the several States, with full power to take into their consideration the defects of this Constitution that have been suggested by the State conventions, and report such amendments thereto as they shall find best suited to promote our common interest and secure to ourselves and our latest posterity the great and unalienable rights of mankind.[12]

After receiving a copy of the Virginia application, the New York legislature followed the Old Dominion's lead and submitted another general call to the Congress for a constitutional convention on May 6, 1789.[13] The third and final petition of the founding era came from Rhode Island in 1790, again requesting a convention to consider revision of the Constitution.[14] The controversial issue of calling a second convention became a moot point, however, when the First Congress under the new Constitution acted quickly to draft and submit to the states twelve amendments. The last ten were ratified and became the Bill of Rights on December 15, 1791.[15]

Four decades passed before another constitutional issue generated two more state petitions to Congress for a convention. In the winter of 1832–33, the nullification crisis prompted South Carolina's legislature to pass resolutions and circulate them among the states calling for "a convention of the States . . . to consider and determine such questions of disputed powers as have arisen between the States of this Confederacy and the General Government." South Carolina also applied to Congress for the convening of this meeting. Only two states responded favorably to the theory advocated by South Carolina (which had taken issue with the high national tariff enacted by Congress) that states had the authority to nullify congressional acts they considered unconstitutional.[16] Georgia petitioned Congress for a general convention; Alabama submitted an application for a convention to address the specific issue of the protective tariff.[17] This nullification theory attracted little support, and some historians even dispute the validity of the South Carolina and Alabama resolutions.[18]

The next wave of petitions occurred on the eve of the Civil War. In an attempt to avert the impending rebellion over slavery, state legislatures in Illinois, Indiana, Kentucky, New Jersey, Ohio, and Virginia, and a convention in Missouri petitioned Congress in 1860 to call a general convention. Nine members of Congress joined these states in requesting a convention to propose amendments aimed at avoiding disunion. The formal convention calls gathered little momentum. As an alternative, Virginia advocated assembling an informal meeting of states to discuss options for maintaining the peace. On February 4, 1861, 136 delegates representing fourteen slave and seven free states convened in Washington to address the constitutional crisis. But the so-called peace convention lacked constitutional authority and the proposed amendments, which it forwarded to Congress, were passed over with little comment.[19]

A month later the peace convention opened its meeting. President Abraham Lincoln, in his first inaugural address, stressed the urgent need for constitutional amendments to resolve the grave national crisis. He stated:

I cannot be ignorant of the fact that many worthy and patriotic citizens are desirous of having the national Constitution amended. While I make no recommendation of amendments, I fully recognize the rightful authority of the people over the whole subject, to be exercised in either of the modes prescribed in the instrument itself; and I should, under existing circumstances, favor rather than oppose a fair opportunity being afforded the people to act upon it. I will venture to add that to me the convention mode seems preferable, in that it allows amendments to originate with the people themselves; instead of only permitting them to take or reject propositions originated by others, not especially chosen for the purpose, and which might not be precisely such as they would wish to accept or refuse.[20]

Lincoln took no action to promote such a gathering and the Civil War made the whole question moot. Petitions in the nation's first century established a pattern of requesting general conventions to address perceived constitutional crises. Some scholars have argued that one explanation for the lack of success of such applications to Congress was the fear that a national convention would be unrestrained in representing the sovereign people. The perception of the "runaway" convention of 1787 inspired these fears.[21]

In his seminal treatise on constitutional conventions published initially in 1867, Judge John A. Jameson addressed the controversy over unlimitable conventions. Using state constitutional conventions as precedents, he argued that whereas legislatures could not "dictate to the Convention what it should, or what it should not recommend," they could establish "general subjects for its consideration." Jameson emphatically delineated the nature of his theoretical limits on constitutional conventions: "In short, it is in general the right and the duty of a legislature to prescribe *when*, and *where*, and *how* a Convention shall meet and proceed with its business, and put its work in operation, but not *what* it shall do."[22] Thus Jameson argued the case for limitable conventions based on the history of state conventions called to address specified topics. Several scholars in the early twentieth century either rejected or modified Jameson's thesis.[23] Nevertheless, his widely disseminated work may have influenced the postbellum pattern of state petitions to Congress for constitutional conventions confined to particular topics.[24]

THE SECOND CENTURY: SPECIFIC CONVENTION CALLS

No state applied for a federal convention between 1861 and 1893. The last decade of the eighteenth century, however, witnessed the initial stirrings of the Progressive Era with its emphasis on direct democracy. The movement inspired a flood of petitions to Congress calling for a convention to consider an amendment allowing the direct election of senators. Between 1894 and 1902, the House of Representatives had passed four resolutions to alter the method of selecting U.S. senators. Not surprisingly, the Senate vetoed the entire quartet of House resolutions calling for popular election to the upper chamber.[25]

The Senate could not block the movement toward direct democracy indefinitely, however. Between 1893 and 1911, thirty states (just one short of the required two-thirds majority) filed a total of seventy-three petitions with Congress to call a convention for proposing the direct-election-of-senators amendment.[26] A reluctant Senate bowed to the tide of public opinion and, on May 13, 1912, adopted a joint resolution with the House proposing the Seventeenth Amendment. By the next May, the states had ratified the amendment and popular election of senators became a constitutional fact.[27]

More than a dozen of the applications to Congress for direct senatorial selection had been included in general convention calls.[28] Although the thirty states that petitioned in the two decades after 1893 lost the battle for a convention, they won the war for the Seventeenth Amendment. The proverbial "handwriting-on-the-wall" syndrome, in which state applications occasionally influenced Congress to take action on an issue, would become a familiar tendency in twentieth-century constitutional revision.[29]

After passage of the Seventeenth Amendment, the states' prerogative to petition Congress was exercised sparingly until the Great Depression. Yet the polygamy issue (generated by Utah's 1896 admission into the Union) had sparked controversy in the early twentieth century and prompted thirty states to request constitutional conventions between 1906 and 1916. The petitions specifically called for a convention to propose an antipolygamy amendment. Even beyond the opposition of some Mormon communities, practical objections to such an amendment surfaced. Some opposition revolved around the potential diminution of traditional state police power in civil law related to marriage. Other opponents believed the issue was unsuited to inclusion in the nation's fundamental law and could be solved by other means. The antipolygamy convention movement fell victim to the passage of time and the inevitable evolution of social mores.

The movement to repeal the unpopular and ineffective Prohibition amendment produced a mere handful of petitions to Congress to call a convention. Instead, the effort to make liquor legal focused on lobbying Congress to propose a repeal amendment and submit it to state conventions for ratification. As noted above, Congress took such a step in 1933, and the era of bootlegging and bathtub gin ended as the nation sank further into the Depression.

The economic emergency of the 1930s spawned another series of convention applications to deal with specific issues. (The last call for a general convention had come in 1929 from Wisconsin.) The first in the series was a single application from California calling for a convention to propose an amendment to allow federal regulation of wages and hours of labor. In 1938 Congress responded to more general pressure in this realm by passing the Fair Labor Standards Act, which established a federal minimum wage, regulated hours worked per week, and set standards for child labor.

A much broader movement in economic matters was launched in 1939 when Maryland and Wyoming became the first two states to call for modification of the Sixteenth Amendment. In reaction to increases in federal income taxes during the 1930s as a means of financing Depression programs, states began to demand a limitation on federal taxing power.[30]

By the end of World War II, eighteen states had joined the bandwagon for petitioning Congress to call a convention to consider the so-called Millionaires' Amendment, modifying the federal government's taxing power. Expenses incurred by the nation during World War II heightened fears over a possible limiting of the government's power to tax. Federal officials presented their reservations to the states, and six rescinded their applications. The Korean War, however, renewed anxiety among opponents of the Sixteenth Amendment who worried that the conflict would cause an increase in federal taxes. Thus by 1952 twelve states had submitted applications to Congress calling for limitation of federal taxing power. Again the movement encountered another stumbling block when interest groups such as labor unions began to oppose the repeal of Amendment Sixteen. Moreover, the income tax debate turned vicious when Representative Wright Patman of Texas labeled the movement "fascist" and cast aspersions on one of its leaders. Still, a total of thirty-eight petitions on this topic reached Congress between 1939 and 1963. But to compound the issue, a dozen of those states rescinded their applications during the same time period.[31]

The 1940s and 1950s witnessed two sets of petitions to Congress for conventions to propose specific amendments related to the presidency. The first series of applications was a reaction to Franklin Roosevelt's unprecedented election to a third term in 1940. Alarmed by his failure to follow the informal two-term tradition established by George Washington and fearful that F.D.R. would run yet again for a fourth term, four states (Illinois, Iowa, Michigan, and Wisconsin) applied for a convention to propose an amendment limiting presidential tenure to two terms. In the same year, 1943, Colorado's and Pennsylvania's legislatures considered petitioning Congress for a similar amendment, but neither adopted the resolution. In 1947 Montana brought the total number of petitions on presidential tenure to five. That same year Congress proposed its own version of the amendment and submitted it to the states, which ratified it as the Twenty-second Amendment by March 1, 1951.[32]

An even briefer set of applications for conventions on presidential treaty-making power reached Congress between 1945 and 1957. Three states requested that a convention consider an amendment to curtail the use of executive agreements by presidents attempting to circumvent constitutionally required Senate participation in the treaty-making process. Despite President Eisenhower's increased utilization of executive agreements in lieu of treaties, the movement to amend the Constitution's provisions for concluding treaties never gained momentum.[33]

One other call for a convention in the immediate postwar era was related to an effort to promote world peace by establishing a global federal government. The State of Florida had sent two petitions to Congress in behalf of this movement—in 1943 and one two years later. In 1949 Florida sent a third application, this time joined by five other states (California, Connecticut, Maine, New Jersey, and North Carolina).[34] The world federal government effort was as idealistic and unrealistic as the Kellogg-Briand Pact's attempt to outlaw war in 1928 and failed to attract any other state support after 1949. Yet its supporters could take some comfort in the establishment of the United Nations.

The impetus for the majority of applications to the Congress requesting a constitutional convention after the mid-1950s was reaction to the liberal activism of the Supreme Court under the leadership of Chief Justice Earl Warren. The Court's 1954 landmark decision in *Brown v. Board of Education,* which outlawed segregation in America's public schools, precipitated the first flood of anti-Court petitions to Congress.

Just one year after *Brown,* Georgia submitted an application for a convention to propose an amendment that would allow *state* control of public education. Indeed, between 1955 and 1961, nine petitions to Congress may be labeled as reactions to the Court's historical decision in *Brown.* They included two additional applications calling for state control of public education (another from Georgia in 1959 and one from Virginia in 1960). Entreaties from three other Southern states (Florida, Louisiana, and Arkansas) requested an amendment relating to Supreme Court decisions in general. Arkansas also submitted a petition in 1959 calling for a convention to reconsider the constitutionality of the Fourteenth Amendment, whose Equal Protection Clause had provided the constitutional basis for the Court's decision in *Brown.* Alabama's 1957 proposal to re-examine the selection process of federal judges was obviously an adverse reaction to the desegregation ruling. Finally, Texas's response included a petition for an amendment to preserve states' rights[35]—a common battle cry among the recalcitrant Southern states in the turbulent decade after the *Brown* ruling.

In another area of constitutional law, Congress was to receive a prophetic application from the State of Indiana in 1957. The Hoosier legislature called for a convention to consider the issue of reapportionment. The United States Supreme Court had sidestepped the controversy over malapportionment of state legislatures when its 1946 decision of *Colgrove v. Green* declared the issue to be a nonjusticiable political question. Nevertheless, in 1962 the Court overturned the *Colgrove* precedent and ruled in *Baker v. Carr* that the judiciary was a proper locus for examining alleged discriminatory legislative apportionment in the states.[36]

The reaction among the states was swift and dramatic. In 1962 the Council of State Governments proposed a constitutional convention to consider several amendments related to the apportionment issue. One called for the removal of apportionment cases from federal jurisdiction. A second proposition would have established a Court of the Union comprised of the fifty state chief justices to hear appeals from U.S. Supreme Court decisions. A third recommendation insisted on a revision of the Article V amendment process to allow bypassing both the congressional and convention method of amendment proposal. Instead, whenever identical texts of an amendment were presented to Congress by two-thirds of the state legislatures, it automatically would be submitted to the states for ratification by a vote of three-fourths of them.[37]

In 1963 a total of twenty-eight states petitioned Congress on behalf of one or more of the Council's three propositions. A dozen states requested a convention on the subject of apportionment per se. Five states expressed their support for the Court of the Union amendment. And the recommendation to amend Article V of the Constitution attracted eleven state applications in 1963.[38]

On the heels of this three-pronged movement came the Court's ruling in the 1964 case of *Reynolds v.Sims,* in which Chief Justice Warren declared for a 6-to-3 Court that *both* houses of a state legislature must be apportioned by the "one-person-one-vote" standard.[39] In the aftermath of this second landmark reapportionment decision, "[t]he Council [of State Governments] renewed its efforts, urging support this time for an amendment which would enable the voters of a state through a referendum to apply the Federal analogy to their legislature by having the representation of one house chosen on some basis other than population."[40] Twenty-eight states responded favorably with petitions to Congress calling for a convention to propose such an amendment. (Nine of the twenty-eight applications were renewals of applications made in 1963.)[41]

Simultaneously, the Senate's Republican minority leader, Everett Dirksen, and thirty-seven cosponsors introduced a resolution for a similar amendment. Two attempts were made, but each time it fell seven votes short of the required two-thirds majority.[42] After the second failure to obtain a congressionally sponsored amendment in 1966, Dirksen vowed to continue the campaign for a convention to propose the apportionment amendment. He argued that it was essential "to preserve in the States the right to determine their own destinies, as far as their legislatures were concerned." He viewed the Supreme Court's application of the "one-man-one-vote" standard to both houses of a state legislature as a usurpation of states' rights. Moreover, he accused opponents of a convention of having "no trust in the people."[43] His chief supporter in the Senate was Nebraska's Roman Hruska, who appealed to his colleagues' self-interest by arguing that the "one-man-one-vote" principle might some day be applied to the Senate "so that there will not be two Senators to each state but representation by population."[44]

Led by Senator Millard Tydings of Maryland, the opposition included in its attack a procedural inquiry regarding the validity of the petitions received up to that time. Tydings argued that applications submitted by state legislatures that the Supreme Court had found to be malapportioned could not possibly be valid, being products of illegally constituted bodies. Moreover, he denied the validity of applications on grounds that twenty-one of the twenty-three malapportioned state legislatures that had submitted apportionment petitions no longer existed. Nineteen already had been reapportioned and new elections held. Two were awaiting new elections.[45]

Senators William Proxmire, Robert Kennedy, and Jacob Javits concurred with Tydings's reasoning, but they also raised another familiar objection to the calling of a convention. The trio maintained that although twenty-nine of the thirty-two applications called for a convention limited to the reapportionment issue, such limitations were not enforceable under the Constitution.[46] Despite the fact that the movement gained a total of thirty-three state applications, just one short of the necessary two-thirds majority, the old fears of an unlimited convention and the death of Senator Everett Dirksen in 1969 scuttled yet another attempt to exercise the Article V amendment procedure.

The Supreme Court precipitated another reactionary set of convention petitions with its church-state rulings in the early 1960s. Its back-to-back decisions in *Engel v. Vitale* (1962) and *Abington Township v. Schempp* (1963) determined that daily recitation of prayers or Bible passages in public schools violated the First Amendment's Establishment Clause. The dual rulings unleashed a storm of protests, including five petitions to Congress over the ensuing decade. In 1963, 1964, and 1966, North Dakota, Massachusetts, and Maryland, respectively, applied for a convention to propose an amendment "to permit prayer in public schools." Arizona's 1972 petition requested that the amendment allow "voluntary prayer" in public schools, and Mississippi's 1973 application expanded the locus of permissible voluntary prayer to include "public buildings."[47]

The calls for a convention on this subject failed, and proposed amendments in Congress have had limited success. In 1984, for example, the Senate rejected proposed constitutional amendments that would have allowed vocal or silent school prayers. More recently, in 1985 the Senate by a decisive vote of 62 to 36 approved a motion to table a bill that would have prohibited federal courts from hearing any case involving prayer in public schools.[48] Yet in 1984, a presidential election year in which the school prayer issue became a prominent campaign theme, Congress passed the Equal Access Act, which makes it unlawful for any public secondary school receiving federal financial assistance "and which has a limited and open forum to deny equal access or a fair opportunity to, or discriminate against, any students who wish to conduct a meeting within that limited open forum on the basis of religious, political, philosophical, or other content of the speech at such meetings."[49]

One year later the Supreme Court dealt school prayer proponents another blow by declaring unconstitutional an Alabama law providing for a "moment of silence" for prayer or meditation in the classroom.[50] In reality, however, compliance with the Supreme Court's school prayer rulings, particularly in the South, has been notably poor.[51]

Only two movements for a convention in the 1960s were unrelated to Supreme Court rulings. One addressed issues regarding presidential selection and succession. In 1963 eight states called for a convention to discuss the long-maligned Electoral College.[52] Although a plethora of studies on reforming or abolishing the Electoral College have been published, the institution remains unchanged a quarter century after the convention call. Presidential succession appeared as an issue on the public agenda after President Eisenhower's numerous illnesses while in office and the assassination of President Kennedy. Congress received three applications regarding an amendment to address such contingencies, but it proposed its own "Appointment of the Vice-President/Presidential Disability" Amendment shortly thereafter. It was ratified as the Twenty-fifth Amendment in 1967.[53]

The 1960s and 1970s also saw renewed concern over federal taxation, but there was a new twist. The concept of returning federal tax revenue to states and localities was one of the fiscal innovations of this period. By 1972 fifteen states had applied to Congress for a convention to consider an amendment on the topic of revenue sharing. As the pressure mounted, Congress enacted the State and Local Fiscal Assistance Act of 1972, which established the General Revenue Sharing program designed to pour billions of federal tax dollars back to state and local governments.[54]

Like the preceding two decades, the 1970s witnessed a number of convention calls in response to civil rights and liberties controversies generated by Supreme Court decisions (see Table 4.1 for a listing of convention calls, 1975–87). Even before the Court handed down its first busing decision, states were responding to the impending litigation on this contentious issue. In 1970 Louisiana and Mississippi applied to Congress to call a convention to propose an antibusing amendment to the Constitution. Their petitions foreshadowed the strident objections one year later when the Supreme Court under its new chief justice, Warren Burger, ruled in a surprisingly unanimous decision that court-ordered busing to achieve racial integration of public schools passed constitutional muster.[55]

One line of opposition surfaced in the Senate, where conservative Democrat Henry Jackson proposed a constitutional amendment that would have proscribed mandatory busing while declaring equal educational opportunities for all. He was joined by traditional Southern Democratic Senators James B. Allen and Sam Ervin, who offered an amendment that would have forbidden assignment of students to public schools on the basis of "race, creed, color or economic class."[56]

Michigan, whose Detroit public schools would be the subject of a Supreme Court busing case in 1974,[57] submitted a petition to Congress calling for a convention to propose an antibusing amendment in 1971. One year later, Tennessee made its application to Congress for a proposed amendment that would have required "the prohibition of Federal interference with neighborhood schools." Mississippi resubmitted an antibusing petition in 1973 and was joined that same year by Nevada, Oklahoma, and Texas.[58]

The campaign against forced busing to achieve racial integration moved to the national political agenda when both major parties included planks regarding busing in their 1972 platforms. Rather predictably for a party headed by George McGovern that year, the Democrats stressed their support for desegregation and the "transportation of students" as a means to that end. Equally predictable, the Republican party platform stated that it was "irrevocably opposed to busing for racial balance." The G.O.P. also wholeheartedly supported President Nixon's Student Transportation Moratorium Act, which called for the immediate cessation of all further court-ordered busing while calling on Congress "to devise permanent new arrangements for assuring desegregated, quality education."[59]

Nevertheless, a number of cities in the 1970s fell under busing orders whose implementation rekindled racial bigotry and violence reminiscent of the previous decade's civil rights movement. In 1979 an antibusing amendment was finally introduced in the House of Representatives. Only the rarely used discharge petition signed by a majority of House members could

Table 4.1

Applications of State Legislatures Received by Congress for Conventions Proposing Amendments to the U.S. Constitution, July 15, 1975–April 24, 1987

Year	STATE	SUBJECT OF CONSTITUTIONAL CONVENTION
1975	Louisiana	Budget balancing
	Kentucky	Compulsory school assignment, prohibition of
	Alabama	Budget balancing
1976	Delaware	Budget balancing
	Georgia	Budget balancing
	Massachusetts	Compulsory school assignment, prohibition of
	Louisiana	Abortions, prohibition of
	Oklahoma	Federal funds, prohibit coercive use by Federal Government.
	S. Carolina	Budget balancing
	Tennessee	Federal funds, prohibit coercive use by Federal Government.
	Virginia	Budget balancing
1977	Arkansas	Abortions, prohibition of
	Indiana	Abortions, prohibition of
	Maryland	Budget balancing
	Massachusetts	Abortions, prohibition of
	New Jersey	Abortions, prohibition of
	Rhode Island	Abortions, prohibition of
	South Dakota	Abortions, prohibition of
	Tennessee	Vetoes, grant President item veto power
	Tennessee	Judges, terms of office of Federal
	Tennessee	Budget balancing
	Utah	Abortions, prohibition of
	Virginia	Vetoes, grant President item veto power
1978	Colorado	Budget balancing
	Delaware	Judicial appointments
	Delaware	Abortions, prohibition of
	Kansas	Budget balancing
	Kentucky	Abortions, prohibition of
	Louisiana	Budget balancing
	Massachusetts	Compulsory school assignment, prohibition of
	Nebraska	Abortions, prohibition of
	Oklahoma	Budget balancing
	Pennsylvania	Abortions, prohibition of
	S. Carolina	Budget balancing
	Tennessee	Budget balancing
	Tennessee	Control of Judiciary
	Wyoming	Budget balancing

Table 4.1 (Continued)

Year	STATE	SUBJECT OF CONSTITUTIONAL CONVENTION
1979	Alabama	Budget balancing
	Arizona	Budget balancing
	Arizona	Business activities, prohibition of Federal government involvement.
	Arkansas	Budget balancing
	Florida	Budget balancing
	Georgia	Abortions, prohibition of
	Idaho	Budget balancing
	Indiana	Budget balancing
	Iowa	Budget balancing
	Louisiana	Budget balancing
	Louisiana	Regulations and rules, Federal
	Maryland	Budget balancing
	Mississippi	Abortions, prohibition of
	Nebraska	Budget balancing
	Nevada	Abortions, prohibition of
	New Hampshire	Abortions, prohibition of
	New Mexico	Budget balancing
	N. Carolina	Budget balancing
	N. Dakota	Budget balancing
	Oregon	Budget balancing
	Pennsylvania	Budget balancing
	S. Dakota	Budget balancing
	Texas	Budget balancing
	Utah	Budget balancing
1980	Alabama	Abortions, prohibition of
	Arizona	Federal funds, prohibit coercive use of
	Idaho	Abortions, prohibition of
	Nevada	Budget balancing
	Oklahoma	Abortions, prohibition of
	Tennessee	Abortions, prohibition of
1981	Alabama	Federal judges, election of
1982	Alaska	Budget balancing
1983	Missouri	Budget balancing
1984	Arizona	Vetoes, grant President item veto power
1986	S. Dakota	Vetoes, grant President item veto power
1987	Utah	Taxes, prohibit Congress from levying on income from obligations of state and local governments

Sources: U.S. Cong., Committee on the Judiciary, Senate, Constitutional Convention Implementation Act of 1984, Report together with Supplemental and Additional Views, 98th Cong., 2nd sess., pp. 56-7. The office of the Secretary of the Senate provided information for 1986-1987.

force the controversial proposal out of committee and onto the floor for a vote. Much to the dismay of busing opponents, the amendment failed to win even a majority of votes, much less the necessary two-thirds majority required for passage. Yet the dispute continued into the next decade with both political parties addressing the issue in their 1980 presidential election platforms. The Democrats reiterated their support for busing but qualified their stand somewhat by calling it "a judicial tool of the last resort." Conversely, the Republican platform repudiated the policy and vowed that "we must halt forced busing" wherever it is in force.[60]

In 1982 Congress approved the so-called Helms Amendment, a rider to the Department of Justice's appropriations bill, which prohibited the department from seeking or favoring court-ordered busing to achieve racial integration. The amendment was consistent with Reagan Administration policy, which supported local school boards that challenged lower court busing orders. During Reagan's first term, the administration merely refused to support busing in new cases. But after its 1984 election mandate, the administration sought actively to halt busing in order to support traditional neighborhood schools but also to return full responsibility for operating schools to local authorities, as was recently done in Norfolk, Virginia.[61]

As the 1980s draw to a close, the next chapter in this saga that began with the *Brown* decision more than thirty years ago will undoubtedly focus on the failure of busing to achieve racial integration in many areas and the ever-changing racial and ethnic composition of urban school districts. The most recent study of school integration patterns reveals that there has been "no significant progress on the desegregation of black students in urban districts since the mid-1970s" and that some areas have shown "severe increases in racial isolation." The next public policy challenge in this realm will be posed by blacks, Hispanics, and Asians who collectively have replaced whites in our major urban areas and who are segregated from each other to a large extent.[62]

In 1973 the Supreme Court handed down what is arguably its most controversial decision of this century. *Roe v. Wade* overturned remaining state laws proscribing abortion. Writing for a 7-to-2 Court, Justice Harry Blackmun argued that the right to privacy "is broad enough to encompass a woman's decision whether or not to terminate her pregnancy." The Court did qualify the woman's right to privacy and thus to an abortion with a three-tiered test that balanced the interests of the woman and the state, depending on the trimester of the pregnancy.

One day before the Court announced its decision in *Roe*, the Indiana legislature petitioned Congress to call a convention to maintain state control over abortion policy. Congress also had anticipated the controversial ruling, and the House of Representatives had debated the issue as early as 1972. Liberal Democratic Representative Bella Abzug led the pro-choice forces. In the upper chamber, Senators James Buckley and Jesse Helms fought on behalf of the antiabortion movement, and Helms introduced an amendment to overturn the Court's decision. In 1973 alone, a total of thirty-two antiabortion amendments were introduced in Congress.[63] Three years later, Congress passed Representative Henry Hyde's resolution prohibiting the use of Medicaid funds for abortions except under very limited circumstances.[64]

Like the busing issue, abortion soon became an integral item on the nation's political agenda. In 1976 both major party platforms addressed the question for the first time. The Republican party vowed to "support the efforts of those who seek enactment of a constitutional amendment to restore protection of the right to life for unborn children." The Democrats, however, stated that "it is undesirable to attempt to amend the U.S. Constitution to overturn Supreme Court decisions in this area."

Throughout the remainder of the 1970s and into the next decade, the abortion controversy made headlines. On each anniversary of the *Roe* decision, antiabortionists have staged boisterous demonstrations in Washington. Presidents Reagan and Bush have addressed the most recent gatherings in a show of support for the right-to-life cause. Not to be outdone, supporters of *Roe* organized a massive march on the nation's capital in the Spring of 1989. The antiabortion faction, however, has been successful in opposing pro-choice candidates for public office. Occasionally, the controversy has turned violent, with the bombing of abortion clinics by fanatical antiabortionists. Yet, for the most part, supporters of abortion were heartened by the Supreme Court's continued bolstering of its original *Roe* decision. But *Webster v. Reproductive Health Services* (1989), in which the Court sanctioned the state of Missouri's various limitations on abortions, placed pro-choice advocates on the defensive.

Article V petitions to Congress have been part of the antiabortionists' strategy. Missouri added its application to Indiana's petition for a convention call on this issue in 1975. Since then, more than a dozen additional states (Alabama, Arkansas, Delaware, Idaho, Kentucky, Louisiana, Massachusetts, Mississippi, Nebraska, New Jersey, Nevada, Oklahoma, Pennsylvania, Rhode Island, South Dakota, Tennessee, and Utah) have submitted petitions to Congress to call a constitutional convention to address the abortion controversy.[65] The four applications from Idaho, Oklahoma, Tennessee, and Alabama, which reached Congress in 1980, reflected the mounting frustration among abortion foes. These states explained their requests for a convention by noting that "the Congress of the United States has not to date proposed . . . a right-to-life amendment."[66]

More recently, in 1983, an amendment outlawing abortion failed in the Senate by a vote of 49 to 50—eighteen votes short of the two-thirds majority needed for passage.[67] Other proposed antiabortion amendments would ban the procedure at all stages of pregnancy and would declare the fetus a "person" under the Constitution and therefore entitled to all constitutional rights. Nevertheless, there are a number of versions of a right-to-life amendment, and forming a consensus around a definitive proposal has been unachievable.[68]

The other prominent movement toward a convention call in the 1980s has centered on an amendment to balance the federal budget. Chapter 7 is devoted to this most recent and nearly successful campaign to convene the only national constitutional convention held since the founding. As a preview, we should note that Indiana in 1957 submitted the first petition to Congress calling for a balanced federal budget.[69] To date, thirty-two applications from states requesting a balanced budget amendment have reached Congress. The total falls two short of the thirty-four states required for congressional action. The effort appears stalled and perhaps moving in reverse since Alabama's recision of its 1976 application in April of 1988.[70] Nevertheless, the issues and questions generated by the movement remain ripe for addressing in Chapter 7.

CONCLUSION: FEAR NOT THE CONVENTION CALL

As this outline of the history of convention calls indicates, those who fear a constitutional convention should be heartened by the unlikelihood of its ever occurring. Indeed, the lack of success of even the most frenetic movements to call a convention is striking. The two-thirds majority required by Article V to trigger Congress' convention call has proved insurmountable over the two centuries since the founding.

Political as well as procedural facts of life have also determined the fate of the applications to Congress to call a convention. On a positive note, Congress has on occasion reacted to state petitions by proposing its own amendments to address a legislative or constitutional need. Certainly, the enactment of the Bill of Rights offers the first illustration of this phenomenon. In the twentieth century, the origin of four amendments to the Constitution may be traced to convention call movements. They include the Seventeenth Amendment (direct election of senators), the Twenty-first Amendment (repeal of Prohibition), the Twenty-second Amendment (limitation of presidential tenure), and the Twenty-fifth Amendment (presidential disability and succession).

Some scholars have concluded that organizers of convention call movements have hoped to pressure Congress to propose its own amendment as an alternative to the much-feared "runaway" convention. Most recently, well over a majority of the thirty-two applications regarding the balanced budget issue actually gave Congress the option of proposing its own amendment or calling a convention to do so.[71] Thus proponents of a failed convention call can still hope for success through congressional proposal of an amendment to address the disputed issue.

Of course, a convention call campaign may incite such political opposition as to preclude both a convention and an amendment proposed by Congress. The antipolygamy movement in the early twentieth century and the effort to repeal the federal income tax amendment failed through congressional inaction. The most recent movements to oppose busing, outlaw abortions, allow school prayer, and promote a balanced federal budget have seen Congress consider but reject possible amendments on each of these topics. As Professor Frank Sorauf has argued, "[T]here is considerable evidence that a slow, late-forming reaction to a petition campaign manages to stall it at the last moment." He notes that as the drive for a convention to propose a balanced budget amendment came within a half-dozen states of the required two-thirds in 1979, opposition began to mount in a number of political forums. Senator Edmund Muskie, chairman of the Senate Budget Committee at the time, and President Jimmy Carter warned of the dangers of a balanced budget amendment in particular and a constitutional convention in general. At the same time, a national assembly of Republican leaders, the National Governors' Association, and the National Conference of State Legislatures all rejected either a balanced budget amendment or a constitutional convention.[72] Thus the balanced budget amendment campaign limped into the 1980s, but its supporters could take heart that at least their pet issue had managed to secure a prominent position on the nation's political agenda.

Another potential barrier for a convention drive relates to the breadth of appeal of the subject addressed in the state applications. Commentator Fred Graham has observed that

[a] large percentage of the state applications Congress has received called for amendments which had very little national support and which would have had no chance of approval by two-thirds of both houses of Congress. Many concerned sectional issues that were too narrow to obtain national support . . . and amounted to little more than state legislatures blowing off political steam.

Graham believes that in the late 1950s states moved beyond attempts at "blowing off steam" to "serious campaigns calculated to amend the Constitution by means of state action." Nevertheless, he notes that radical proposals, regardless of the seriousness of their drafters' intentions, have failed to clear the hurdles imposed by Article V—hurdles meant to ensure broad national support for constitutional changes.[73]

Thus the republican mechanisms enshrined in the Constitution have operated as James Madison argued they would in *Federalist* No. 10. Our extended republic with its representative institutions has served to thwart the unwise or unjust efforts, particularly of minority factions, to amend the nation's governing document.[74]

NOTES

1. As quoted in Herman V. Ames, *Proposed Amendments to the Constitution of the United States during the First Century of Its History* (New York: Burt Franklin, 1970), pp. 301–302.

2. Wilbur Edel, *A Constitutional Convention: Threat or Challenge?* (New York: Praeger, 1981), p. 1.

3. Paul J. Weber, "The Constitutional Convention: A Safe Political Option," *Journal of Law and Politics* 3 (Winter 1986), 57.

4. Kermit Hall, Harold M. Hyman, and Leon V. Sigal, eds., *The Constitutional Convention as an Amending Device* (Washington, DC: American Political Science Association and American Historical Association, 1981), p. 114.

5. Ames, *Proposed Amendments*, p. 282.

6. Winton U. Solberg, ed., *The Federal Convention and the Formation of the Union* (Indianapolis: Bobbs-Merrill, 1958), pp. 366, 375.

7. Ibid., pp. 366–375.

8. See Chapter 3 supra.

9. Linda C. Healy, "Past and Present Convention Calls: From Gay Abandon to Cautious Resistance," paper presented at Southern Political Science Association Meeting, Savannah, GA., November 1, 1984, pp. 2–3.

10. Ibid.

11. Ames, *Proposed Amendments*, p. 310.

12. *American State Papers*, 037, Doc. 4.

13. Ibid., Doc. 5.

14. Fred P. Graham, "The Role of the States in Proposing Constitutional Amendments," *American Bar Association Journal* 49 (December 1963), 1179.

15. Solberg, *The Federal Convention*, pp. 376–379.

16. Philip L. Martin, "The Application Clause of Article Five," *Political Science Quarterly* 85 (December 1970), 619–620.

17. Graham, "The Role of the States," p. 1178.

18. Martin, "The Application Clause," p. 619.

19. Ibid., p. 620; Ames, *Proposed Amendments*, p. 283.

20. Quoted in John T. Noonan, Jr., "The Wisdom of the Constitutional Convention Method," *Congressional Record* 125 (May 3, 1979), 9841.

21. Martin, "The Application Clause," p. 621.

22. John A. Jameson, *A Treatise on Constitutional Conventions, Their History, Powers, and Modes of Processing*, 2nd ed. (Chicago: E. B. Myers, 1869), p. 353 (original emphasis).

23. See Walter Dodd, *The Revision and Amendment of State Constitutions* (Baltimore: 1910); Roger S. Hoar, *Constitutional Conventions: Their Nature, Powers, and Limitations* (Boston: Little, Brown, 1917); and Francis H. Heller, "Limiting a Constitutional Convention: The State Precedents," *Cardozo Law Review* 3 (1982), 563.

24. This hypothesis was suggested by Healy, "Past and Present Convention Calls," p. 6.

25. Martin, "The Application Clause," pp. 621–622.

26. Healy, "Past and Present Convention Calls," p. 7; Noonan, "The Wisdom of the Constitutional Method," p. 9843; Martin,"The Application Clause," p. 622.

27. Martin, "The Application Clause," p. 622.

28. Graham, "The Role of the States," pp. 1179–1181.

29. Hall and Hyman, *The Constitutional Convention*, p. 115.

30. Barbara Prager and Gregory Milmoe, "Article V Applications Submitted Since 1789," in *Amendment of the Constitution by the Convention Method Under Article V* (Chicago: American Bar Association, 1974), p. 73.

31. Martin, "The Application Clause," pp. 625–626, fn. 30; Healy, "Past and Present Convention Calls," pp. 8–9.

32. Healy, "Past and Present Convention Calls," p. 9.

33. Ibid., p. 10.

34. Graham, "The Role of the States," pp. 1181–1182.

35. Ibid., p. 1182.

36. Henry J. Abraham, *Justices and Presidents: A Political History of Appointments to the United States Supreme Court*, 2nd ed. (New York: Oxford University Press, 1985), p. 265.

37. Martin, "The Application Clause," p. 624.

38. Graham, "The Role of the States," pp. 1182–1183.

39. Abraham, *Justices and Presidents*, pp. 257–258.

40. Martin, "The Application Clause," p. 625.

41. Ibid.

42. Ibid.

43. As quoted in Edel, *A Constitutional Convention*, p. 87.

44. Ibid., p. 88.

45. Ibid., pp. 88–89.

46. Ibid., pp. 89–90.

47. Healy, "Past and Present Convention Calls," p. 13.

48. "Senate Rejects Bill to Permit School Prayer," *Congressional Quarterly Weekly Report*, 43, No. 37, September 14, 1985, 1842.

49. *New York Times*, July 7, 1984, p. A16.

50. *Wallace v. Jaffree*, 472 U.S. 38 (1985).

51. Abraham, *The Judicial Process: An Introductory Analysis of the Courts of the United States, England, and France*, 5th ed. (New York: Oxford University Press, 1986), p. 241.

52. Graham, "The Role of the States," 1182.

53. Healy, "Past and Present Convention Calls," p. 12.

54. Ibid., pp. 12–13.

55. *Swann v. Charlotte-Mecklenburg Bd. of Ed.*, 402 U.S. 1 (1971); see Abraham, *Justices and Presidents*, p. 296.

56. Edel, *A Constitutional Convention*, p. 60.

57. *Millikin v. Bradley*, 418 U.S. 717 (1974).

58. Healy, "Past and Present Convention Calls," p. 14.

59. As quoted in Edel, *A Constitutional Convention*, pp. 60–61.

60. Ibid., p. 61.

61. Joel B. Grossman and Richard S. Wells, *Constitutional Law and Judicial Policy Making*, 3rd ed. (New York: Longman, 1988), pp. 316–317.

62. New findings on this problem appear in a study by Gary Orfield and Franklin Montford entitled "Racial Change and Desegregation in Large School Districts"; see the *New York Times*, June 23, 1988, p. A16, for an account of this project conducted for the National School Boards Association.

63. Edel, *A Constitutional Convention*, p. 64.

64. Grossman and Wells, *Constitutional Law*, p. 674.

65. Healy, "Past and Present Convention Calls," p. 15.

66. As quoted in Edel, *A Constitutional Convention*, p. 65.

67. "High Court to Re-examine State Abortion Regulations," *Congressional Quarterly Weekly Report*, 43, No. 43, October 26, 1985, 2153.

68. Healy, "Past and Present Convention Calls," p. 15.

69. Graham, "The Role of the States," p. 1182.

70. *Congressional Quarterly Weekly Report,* 46, No. 22, May 28, 1988, 1443.

71. Hall, Hyman, and Sigal, *The Constitutional Convention,* pp. 115–116.

72. Ibid., pp. 116–117.

73. Graham, "The Role of the States," 1176.

74. James Madison, *Federalist* No. 10, in *The Federalist Papers,* Clinton Rossiter, ed. (New York: Mentor Books, 1961), pp. 77–84.

5

WHAT STATE CONVENTIONS CAN TEACH US

THROUGH 1989, MORE than 230 state constitutional conventions have assembled in the United States.[1] Even within the state context, circumstances vary enough to make comparisons problematic. And to try to apply state precedents to a future convention at the federal level is perhaps to engage in the proverbially futile exercise of comparing apples and oranges. As one commentator on constitutional conventions has expressed it, "No two states, no two conventions, no two referenda, no two political situations of whatever kind are likely to be found that are exactly alike."[2] Yet certain uniformities may exist regardless of the context. This chapter is devoted to discovering and examining the universals that may obtain at both governmental levels of constitutional revision.

Initially, we must confront the different nature of constitutionalism at state and national levels. Statistics paint a brilliant distinction between frequency of constitutional revision and amendment of state constitutions and the federal document. Since adoption, the U.S. Constitution has been formally amended twenty-six times, the first ten of those changes embodying the Bill of Rights. In contrast, as of 1987, the fifty states had adopted a total of 5,366 amendments to their constitutions! (A total of 8,554 amendments had been submitted to voters for consideration.) Moreover, six states each have adopted half a dozen or more constitutions during their respective histories. Louisiana holds the distinction of having accepted the most constitutions—eleven in all.[3]

The contrast between the amount of verbiage in the U.S. Constitution and in state charters is also illustrative. The former is a model of brevity at just over 9,000 words, including amendments. Conversely, most state constitutions are at least twice that long. Indeed, the Alabama constitution tops the list with well over 170,000 words, including its staggering 471 amendments.[4]

As the statistics suggest, the substance of constitutions at the federal and state levels is strikingly different. In general, amendments to the U.S. Constitution have been confined to constitutional issues such as fundamental rights, suffrage, tenure of office, and filling vacancies in constitutional offices. At the state level, however, the plethora of amendments has resulted from efforts to address public policy needs in addition to constitutional exigencies. As Professor Elmer Cornwell has correctly argued, "[C]onstitutional revision has become, at the state level, far more than at the national, a major *political* process which is closely related to and tends to supplement the normal legislative processes."[5]

Finally, a structural difference exists to differentiate the amending processes at the state and federal levels. States, as autonomous units, do not have to consider questions related to federalism in amending their constitutions. On the other hand, national constitutional revision is closely tied to the issue of federalism, reflected in Article V of the Constitution.[6]

Yet despite the very real procedural and substantive differences between state and national constitutional revision, parallels exist; and state constitutional conventions provide a wealth of precedents for planning and organizing a federal constitutional assembly. Scholars and politicians have consistently raised a number of questions about federal conventions.[7] They most often relate to the calling of the convention, election of delegates, and the organization of the convention. State convention precedents do not provide definitive answers to each and every query. Nevertheless, the history of state conventions sheds light on a number of controversies over the convening of a national meeting under Article V provisions for amending the U.S. Constitution.

CALLING A CONVENTION

A cluster of questions in this category relates to the initiation and authorization of the convention call. At these initial stages in the process, differences in the state and federal mechanisms are apparent. Table 5.1 reveals the contrasts and parallels in the two convention structures:[8]

Table 5.1
Convention Structures: Contrasts and Parallels

STAGE	STATE MECHANISM	FEDERAL MECHANISM
Initiation	Legislature	Informal movement
Authorization	Popular vote	⅔ of states
Calling	Legislature (and electorate)	Congress (and states or electorate)
Proposal of amendments	Convention	Convention
Ratification	Popular vote	¾ of states

Most of the forty-one states whose constitutions provide for constitutional conventions require legislative submission of the convention question to the voters before enactment of enabling legislation.[9] Thus the usual state system of initiating and authorizing a constitutional convention is more certain than the same stage at the federal level. The lack of an institutionalized initiation system at the national level often ensures confusion and disorganization on the part of movements to call for a convention.[10] Moreover, the requirement that two-thirds of the states submit applications to Congress for convening a convention has resulted in questions regarding the validity of such petitions.

The criteria for determining a valid application remain unclear. In addition, there are questions relating to who should determine validity and whether a state may rescind its application. Freed from the constrictions of federalism and the burden of coping with fifty separate government entities, states have no need to address the type of uncertainties raised at the national level.

State precedent, however, does offer some understanding of the question of what happens if Congress refuses to act on a valid call by two-thirds of the states for a constitutional convention. As depicted in Table 5.1, the usual steps leading to the calling of a *state* constitutional convention entail (1) action by the state legislature to submit the question of calling a convention to the people, (2) a positive vote by the electorate, (3) the legislative enactment of enabling legislation to provide for the election of convention delegates and operation of the convention, and (4) the election of the delegates.[11] Thus the problem of a recalcitrant legislature is rare at the state level because the legislative body usually initiates the convention procedure itself.

Yet to circumvent a balking legislature at the outset, fourteen states now require asking voters at fixed intervals if a constitutional convention should be called. Eight states provide for submission of the convention question to the electorate every twenty years; one state, every sixteen; four states, every ten years; and one state, every nine years.[12] Thus the state and national procedures have become more similar in that the trend in state constitutions is to bypass legislative initiation of the convention call. But as Professor Robert Martineau has written in his examination of mandatory referenda on calling a state constitutional convention: "Whenever the convention issue is submitted pursuant to a constitutional directive but the actual holding of a convention is dependent upon legislative action, there is always the risk that the legislature will not comply with its duty to see that a convention is held."[13] Indeed, before 1970, Martineau unearthed eight instances of state legislatures failing to call conventions even after a majority of the electorate voting on the convention question cast favorable votes. In three of the eight examples, the legislature simply refused to pass enabling legislation. In five instances, the state constitutional provisions were interpreted to require a majority voting in favor of a convention greater than a simple majority of those voting on the question. On another occasion, the state legislature of New York delayed calling a convention for eight years even after the people had voted for an assembly.[14]

What remedies for legislative recalcitrance have been suggested at the state level? Martineau has noted the long-accepted principle that the courts have no power to force a legislature to act. Among the theories on which this principle has been based is the view that a writ of mandamus, by which a court orders the performance of an obligatory duty, could not force the legislature to pass legislation, which necessarily involves the exercise of discretion. Furthermore, the powerlessness of courts in such disputes has been supported by separation-of-powers assertions, namely, that one branch of government cannot interfere with another branch in the exercise of duties exclusively assigned by the Constitution to the latter.[15]

Despite the legal precedents favoring the impotence of the judiciary in these matters, several recent cases have suggested alternative interpretations that provide justification for a court to enforce the popular vote for a state constitutional convention. For example, in 1960 the Kentucky Court of Appeals ruled that once the electorate had voted for a convention, the legislature had a "ministerial duty enjoined upon it by the constitution in the execution of a public mandate."[16] Furthermore, the Kentucky court opined that the "choice of whether a constitutional convention shall be called rests entirely with the electorate. The discretion of the legislature is at an end when the matter is finally proposed."[17] The terms "ministerial" and "discretion" are significant because they are crucial to the issuance of a writ of mandamus.[18]

A second argument relates to the asserted fundamental right of the people to reform their government. But even if the right is indeed fundamental, as the Declaration of Independence and some state constitutions would indicate, can it be subsumed under federal constitutional rights as described by the U.S. Supreme Court in *Baker v. Carr*? If so, then the "limitations of justiciability, political question, and separation of powers do not apply to a suit alleging that a federal constitutional right has been violated by a refusal by a state legislature to act."[19] If the federal fundamental rights argument obtains for refusal of *state* legislatures to call a convention duly voted upon by the electorate, it would seemingly be more likely to apply to the refusal of Congress to call a *federal* convention.

Nevertheless, the U.S. Supreme Court would have to overturn its 1939 precedent of *Coleman v. Miller*,[20] which excluded the judicial branch from Article V disputes on grounds that they were nonjusticiable political questions. Although *Baker v. Carr* and its progeny narrowed the scope of the political question doctrine, some scholars argue that the Court would continue to sidestep any controversy over the refusal by Congress to call a convention requested by the required two-thirds of the states. As Arthur Bonfield has asserted,

judicial review on the merits of state legislative apportionment or the drawing of congressional districts by the states only involves federal judicial superintendence of state action or inaction; but judicial review of Congress' failure to call an Article V convention directly involves the federal courts in an effort to force its co-equal branch of the Government to perform a duty exclusively entrusted to it by the Constitution.[21]

Yet the reasoning in the 1960 Kentucky precedent coupled with the fundamental rights argument would provide a possible basis on which the Court could overturn *Coleman* if it were so inclined.

One of the most frequently addressed questions is whether, if a convention is called, Congress can limit it in terms of topics and duration. One scholar, Professor Francis Heller, has argued that state precedents on this question are inapplicable at the national level. Heller, however, examined a related but slightly different issue. He raised the question of whether *states* may limit a national convention in their petitions to Congress calling for one. For example, the most recent rash of applications to Congress for a convention has confined such a meeting to matters related to a balanced budget amendment. Heller maintains that state judicial precedents have allowed citizens of a state to limit state constitutional conventions by approving the limitations through a popular vote. The underlying principle for the precedents is the recognized discretion of the sovereign to delegate power in limited portions.[22]

Heller argues that federalism considerations at the national level render state precedents inappropriate. He writes, "Since the question of limitability has profound implications with regard to the balance of power between the federal and state governments, federalism concerns, and not concerns of the delegation of sovereign power, should control."[23] In other words, because state convention procedures do not have to consider federalism questions, the precedents for calling conventions do not apply to the Article V procedures, which are based on a federal system.[24]

Moreover, Heller notes the practical inability to replicate state precedents at the national level. In states, the people exercise their sovereignty by voting on the constitutional convention. They delegate a portion of their sovereignty in approving a limited convention. Heller believes that the popular vote for approving a convention call finds no analogue at the national level. Therefore, the sovereign people cannot participate at the national level nor delegate limited power to a convention.[25]

Others have interpreted state precedents as supporting the possibility of either Congress or the states or both placing limitations on a national convention.[26] But to arrive at such a conclusion is to interpret the locus of sovereignty differently than Heller does.[27] Thus it has been argued that states play the same roles at the same stages of a federal constitutional convention as are played by the electorate in state conventions. Within their respective spheres, the states and the electorate are responsible for authorization and ratification of constitutional conventions and their output. Such a view of the convention process implies that the states are sovereign in the United States as the people are in the states. Of course, this interpretation appears to run afoul of post–Civil War constitutional dogma regarding sovereignty in the United States. But as has been pointed out by Professor Charles Black, Article V is not a twentieth-century creation but rather a product of the 1787 convention, at which "the states were in a position of at least nominal sovereignty, and were considering whether to unite."[28]

Moreover, even as Heller notes, the British legal philosopher

John Austin maintained that the power to amend the constitution is the essence of sovereignty. By this reasoning, sovereignty inheres in the amending body. "Insofar as the convention clause may be said to give the (*united*) states power both necessary and sufficient to amend the Constitution, some have proclaimed the states united as sovereign in the United States."[29] If the sovereign is defined as whoever has the last word, then the Founders gave that role to the states, not Congress, in Article V's provisions for amending the Constitution. Indeed, it was the staunch Antifederalist George Mason who had passionately and successfully argued in favor of state initiation of the amendment procedure as a check on the feared abuses by the national congress.[30]

To summarize the argument supporting potential state limits on a national convention, if the states were intended to be the final authority under Article V just as the people fulfill such a role at the state level, then it follows that the states (like the electorate) may delegate a portion of their sovereignty to limit a constitutional convention at the federal level.[31]

One of the classic treatises on conventions arrives at a similar conclusion, namely, that such assemblies may be limited, but does so by another syllogistic route. Judge John A. Jameson, writing to support the concept of the limited convention in the 1860s, premised his theory on what he termed the "quasi" sovereignty of the people of the United States. In Jameson's view, the "real sovereign" was the American nation. Its will was to be expressed "authentically" by the legislature "in relation to all emergencies of the social state."[32] Therefore, the constitutional convention, created by the legislature, was subordinate to it and likewise to the will of the sovereign nation as expressed through the Congress.[33] Jameson concluded, on the issue of a limitable convention, that it "is in no proper sense of the term and to no extent sovereign"; rather "it is but an agency employed by the sovereign to institute government."[34]

Ultimately, the key to determining whether or not a federal constitutional convention could be limited and if so by whom depends on the interpretation of the locus of sovereignty. Certainly there is a persuasive body of political theory to support the limitability of conventions at both levels of government. Some state courts have asserted that delegates to such limited assemblies "are but agents of the people, are restricted to the exercise of the powers conferred upon them by the law which authorizes their selection and assemblage."[35] Thus political theory and legal precedent exist for limiting the scope of a constitutional convention.[36]

ELECTION OF DELEGATES

The next obvious step subsequent to the calling of a constitutional convention entails the selection of delegates. States have had to determine who would be eligible to serve as a delegate, and their previous decisions may offer guidelines for the nation in making such determinations for a future national convention.

The state of Illinois offers one example of determining eligibility for delegates to a state convention. Article XIV, Section 1 of its constitution provides that the qualification of delegates to a constitutional convention "shall be the same as that of members of the Senate."[37] Such qualifications include U.S. citizenship, the attainment of twenty-five years of age, and five years' residency in the state and two years in the district from which they are elected. Furthermore, a senator-elect to the Illinois General Assembly cannot hold "any lucrative office" in the Illinois, United States, or any foreign government when he or she takes the seat in the Senate. Thus a delegate to an Illinois convention may not hold a seat in the House or Senate of the Illinois General Assembly or any other compensated government office—Illinois, United States or foreign—when taking his or her seat as a convention delegate.[38]

Conversely, Arkansas took a different approach to delegate qualifications. In a 1970 Arkansas case, *Harvey v. Ridgeway*, the court held that participation in a constitutional convention was not similar to employment in any other office in the state. The court declared that a convention is equal to and independent of existing branches of government.[39] Thus the court found no conflict in any dual employment as a convention delegate and an employee of a particular branch of government. Senator David Pryor of Arkansas, who made the above information available in a 1979 hearing before the Senate Judiciary Committee's Subcommittee on the Constitution, concluded that he saw no reason "why any individual needs to be excluded from the pool of minds available to assist in the drafting of a new amendment."[40]

There is certainly adequate precedent for multiple membership. Twenty-one of the original fifty-five members elected to the Constitutional Convention of 1787 were past or active members of the Continental Congress. Nine members, including James Madison, were active members of both bodies. Edmund Randolph was both governor of Virginia and a convention delegate. Madison had the further distinction, as did several other delegates, of also being members of a state ratifying convention!

Idealistically, one would hope that a constitutional convention, at either level of government, would attract the best minds, the most experienced public servants, and the least politically motivated delegates. Of course, experience at the state level suggests that the model set of delegates rarely, if ever, gathers at constitutional conventions.

Research by Professor Cornwell indicates that delegates to past state conventions can be categorized under three general labels based on motivation. The first grouping typifies the dedicated reformer who indeed has a public service orientation. Such a public servant is committed to the goals of constitutional reform rather than to feathering his or her own political nest.

A second category describes those less altruistic delegates who seek election to a constitutional convention in order to represent and protect a vested interest. This category includes delegates with a variety of backgrounds including legislators, party officials, local officeholders, judges, labor union members, farmers, conservationists, and members of special interest groups.

A third category is reserved for purely self-interested individuals who are attempting to boost a new or faltering political career. A study of the 1943–44 constitutional convention in Missouri noted that the "career ambitions frequently were concealed in the verbal and voting reactions of particular delegates."[41] An observer of Hawaii's statehood convention commented that election to the assembly meant that "opportunity was presented for the 'has been' to attempt a political comeback and for the newcomer to test his voting strength." In fact, "some were catapulted to positions of prominence which augured well for subsequent political careers." One delegate at Maryland's 1968 convention could not help observing rather pointedly, "A lot of politicians are being born around here."[42]

Undoubtedly, some self-selection must occur among those who choose to seek delegate positions. Philip Schrag, a law professor at Georgetown University and ultimately a delegate to the 1982 constitutional convention that drafted a constitution for the proposed statehood of the District of Columbia, undertook some agonizing soul-searching before entering the delegate election. Although he had not been part of the original group that had proposed the project, he had joined the informal debates over D.C. statehood at an early stage. Moreover, he reasoned that he had every right to run for office in an open, public election. He also knew that he was an enthusiastic supporter of statehood for the nation's capital. The proposed state would indubitably elect black, Democratic, liberal, pro-urban senators, with whose agenda Schrag knew he would agree wholeheartedly.[43]

Schrag examined his own qualifications and decided that his law degree and his experience in drafting legislation would be much-needed skills at the convention. Before making a final decision, he consulted an unnamed source who could offer experienced observations on District politics. Schrag recounts the intriguing and somewhat startling insight he received from his anonymous adviser:

"Don't do it," my source says. "It could be a disaster for you."

I am surprised. "What do you mean? I think I would have a chance of winning."

"That's the problem," he says. "It doesn't matter if you lose. The headache is winning."

"If you go to that convention," my source tells me, "the resentment against you will be terrible. You're white, you're male, and you live in Ward Three. That's three strikes against you for openers. But worse than that, you're articulate, you have speaking and writing skills that many of the others don't have. They'll depend on you to some extent, and they'll hate you for it."

"And to top it off, you teach at Georgetown. You'll be identified with it. There'll probably be gays at the convention, who will hate the University because of the Catholic Church's line on homosexuality."

"You didn't mention that I'm Jewish, " I jest. Half-jest.

"That, too, " he says. "I didn't want to say it, but they'll be more circumspect about that. It won't be as clear."[44]

So much for the idealized convention!

Obviously, conventions are comprised of delegates with an infinite number of axes to grind. Cornwell has offered some wisdom on the most successful mix of delegates based on his research of state precedents. Altruistic reformers may be considered "blue ribbon" types; but if they constitute the majority of a convention, an unratifiable document might result, because reformers often are unwilling to accommodate political realities. For example, Maryland's 1967–68 convention produced a model constitution that went down to a crushing defeat at the hands of the electorate. Conversely, a convention dominated by vested political interests (particularly those represented by legislators) may be too willing to preserve the status quo.[45] No one can determine with statistical precision the most propitious mix necessary for a successful convention, but state convention histories are helpful in illustrating potential pitfalls in types of delegates selected.

Having discussed delegate eligibility and qualifications, we turn to the issue of elections for delegates to constitutional conventions. There are several questions that have been raised regarding selection procedures for a national convention. For example, must delegates be specially elected? Could Congress simply appoint its own members? Are the states to be equally represented, or must the one-person, one-vote rule apply?

Jameson's comprehensive tome on constitutional conventions made uncharacteristically short shrift of the question on who should select convention delegates. He wrote,

The legislature . . . is the proper body to direct the election and assembling of the Convention. Common sense would indicate that delegates intended to represent, first, the electoral body, and, through that, the sovereign, if they are to represent truly the different phases of opinion current among the people at large, should be chosen by the entire electoral body.[46]

Of course, the electoral procedure issue is far more complex than Jameson's simple declaration. The precedent at the state level is popular election of delegates in special elections. (Unlike at the national level, however, states usually ask for popular confirmation of convention calls, and delegate selection often occurs simultaneously.)[47]

If the United States were to hold a convention, the next hurdle would be determining the bases of election for delegates. In the twenty-seven state constitutional conventions held between 1938 and 1968, most delegates were elected from state representative, state senatorial, or congressional districts. In addition, some members were elected at large and a few were ex-officio members.[48] At the state level, the combination of district and at-large selection has been called the most feasible approach because it not only provides representation on a population basis but also attempts to insure representation for the various economic, social, and geographical interests of a state.[49]

Apportionment of delegates would undoubtedly pose one of the most contentious issues for a national convention, as it has at the state level. As the National Municipal League noted in its manual for state conventions, "Determining the apportionment of delegates can be the most important action in the whole process of constitutional revision by convention."[50] An inequitable system of apportionment can result in biases toward various groups, which would render the product of the convention suspect. Thus at the state level, the call has been for delegate seats to be apportioned as nearly as possible on the one-person, one-vote principle. In this postreapportionment era, it is more than likely that the same standard would be demanded of a national convention.

In fact, the American Bar Association's Special Constitutional Convention Study Committee recommended that for a national convention, each state should be allotted the number of delegates equal to its representation in the House of Representatives in order to approximate one-person, one-vote requirements. Yet, the committee admitted that such a system would result in deviations of up to 50 percent resulting from the fact that each state would be entitled to a delegate regardless of population. Nevertheless, redistricting the entire nation for a delegate election was pronounced unfeasible and unrealistic.[51]

There are also some lessons to be learned from state experiences regarding partisanship in delegate selection. In general, the options in this realm may be categorized as follows:

1. Partisan selection, including party primaries, as used for the conventions held in New York in 1967, Michigan in 1961–62, and Illinois in 1920–22.

2. Bipartisan selection, in which each of the two major political parties is guaranteed an equal number of delegates, as was used for the conventions held in New Jersey in 1947 and 1966, Connecticut in 1965, and Missouri in 1943.

3. Nonpartisan selection, in which candidates run without party designation, as used for conventions held in Maryland in 1967–68, Alaska in 1955–56, and Hawaii in 1950.[52]

The above examples offer a mixed bag of results. The Illinois convention of 1920–22 was dominated by Republicans who wrote into the new constitution apportionment provisions that were unfavorable to the state's Democrats. The Cook County Democratic machine was instrumental in engineering the defeat of the proposed constitution. Likewise, a proposed New York constitution of 1967, a product of a partisan convention, suffered rejection at the hands of the voters. Michigan's 1961–62 convention adopted a new constitution along party lines. The state's Republicans had held a two-to-one majority at the convention and incurred the wrath of Michigan Democrats, the AFL-CIO, and the NAACP. The new constitution squeaked through the ratification election by a bare majority of 50.2 percent.[53]

In general, partisan conventions are prone to codifying in their constitutions material more appropriate to ordinary legislation. This result is particularly likely when the minority party in the state government as a whole manages to elect a majority of delegates and proceeds to write its pet legislative programs into the new constitution. Parties, by their nature, are arguably more responsive to special interest group demands to enshrine ordinary policy in the state's governing document.[54]

The products of all four bipartisan conventions noted above were approved by the voters. The two most recent examples, however, were limited to the reapportionment issue and were following the one-person, one-vote mandate of the U.S. Supreme Court. Conversely, the successful New Jersey convention of 1947 specifically avoided the contentious reapportionment problem. The results of these conventions in terms of inclusion of legislative material are mixed. The 1947 New Jersey constitution was relatively concise, approximately 16,000 words. On the other hand, Missouri's document produced at the 1943 convention ran approximately 40,000 words. Perhaps the most severe drawback to bipartisan delegate selection is the failure to represent the growing number of independent voters throughout the United States.[55]

Nonpartisan state conventions held during this century have compiled an impressive record of effecting substantial constitutional reforms that won acceptance by the electorate. Nebraska (1919–20), Massachusetts (1917–19), and Ohio (1912) wrote new constitutions that were ratified by voters during the Progressive Era. Rhode Island's conventions in 1944, 1951, 1955, and 1958, and the statehood assemblies in Alaska and Hawaii, all nonpartisan convocations, met with success. The product of Maryland's 1967–68 convention was singularly unsuccessful for some of the reasons noted earlier.[56] On the whole, however, it appears that organizers of a national convention should be aware of the relative strengths of nonpartisan delegate selection as demonstrated by state precedents.

THE CONVENTION PROCESS

Questions have been raised about the power of Congress to include specific rules for the operation of a convention if it were to call one. If Congress could attach rules, would the convention be obliged to follow them? What would be the consequences if it did not? Appendix I contains a specific set of rules proposed by a Senate subcommittee but never adopted. Such rules may be theoretically sound, but would they work in practice?

More than a century ago, Jameson wrote that "[t]he call under which a Convention assembles may contain specific directions in reference to its organization, in which case, it will be the duty of the body to follow those directions to the letter."[57] He added that no call for a convention had ever attempted to constrain an assembly with "minute regulations." In fact, up to the time he wrote his treatise in 1869, most convention calls had confined themselves to prescribing the time and method of electing delegates, the qualifications of the electors, the time of assembling the convention, and various other organizational matters that naturally required legislative attention before the convention could meet.[58]

Attempts by a legislature to place procedural limits on a convention could be problematic. On the state level such limitations (i.e., directives on record-keeping, printing of convention records, etc.) have usually been struck down. One state court ruled that a convention "has full control of all its proceedings."[59] Other precedents imply that a convention may legally ignore external efforts to control its internal procedures.[60]

Questions of substantive limitations on conventions may be even more controversial and complex, as indicated earlier in this chapter. Substantive limitations may be inclusive, exclusive, or both. They may include one or more topics to be addressed and/or they may exclude certain subjects from consideration. New Jersey's post–World War II conventions are illustrative of each type of substantive limitation. Its convention in 1947 was directed to examine any area in the constitution for possible reform *except* apportionment of the state legislature; the convention nineteen years later was proscribed from considering any subject *other than* apportionment.[61]

Professor Albert Sturm found that between 1938 and 1968 legislatures tended to favor limited conventions presumably because they are more easily controlled than conventions with unlimited agendas. During that time period, state legislatures in Rhode Island, Virginia, and Tennessee supported calls for limited conventions. In Michigan, however, the state legislature refused to fund preparations for the unlimited convention of 1961–62 and balked at providing financing for delegate salaries and other convention expenses. Yet during the three decades after 1938, twenty-three unlimited conventions were held, compared to nine limited assemblies. The success of the products of the unlimited conventions was split almost evenly, with twelve constitutions approved and eleven defeated. Limited conventions, however, registered eight approvals and only one defeat.[62]

Table 5.2 indicates that over the past decade and a half, state conventions with no substantive limitations have outnumbered limited conventions by a margin of 3 to 2:[63]

Table 5.2
Number of Unlimited/Limited Conventions (1971–86)

Unlimited conventions	Limited conventions
Montana (1971–72)	Louisiana (1973)
North Dakota (1971–72)	Rhode Island (1973)
New Hampshire (1974–84)	Texas (1974)
Arkansas (1978–80)	Tennessee (1977)
Hawaii (1978)	
Rhode Island (1986)	

Finally, we must address the issue of whether state conventions have ever run away. Of the 230 state conventions, it can reasonably be argued that six overrode limitations placed on them, the last one being in 1908.[64] Yet the use of limitations at the state level has been successful on the vast majority of occasions and should be viewed as a viable option for an Article V convention, especially, as we note later, because a convention can only *propose* amendments. States must still ratify them.

It is probably on the matter of organizational details that state precedents are most instructive for a future national convention. The numerous commentaries on past state conventions stress the need for careful preparation prior to convening a constitutional assembly. Convention planners should insist on scholarly studies of the substantive issues to be addressed by the delegates. In addition, convention strategists must research the political context in which the constitution is to be revised.[65]

The District of Columbia statehood convention was preceded by a seminar for delegates at Georgetown University. Although delegate Philip Schrag praised the substance and utility of the law lectures, he and his colleagues were impatient to hear strategies for organizing their convention before it actually met for the first time.[66]

As indicated above, state legislatures have been responsible for funding preliminary research for conventions, delegate salaries and expenses, and other basic convention costs. Appropriations have varied widely for state conventions.[67] Rhode Island's 1986 convention received an initial appropriation of just $50,000, but it was later augmented by a $335,965 appropriation. The convention eventually spent $333,622. Since the early 1970s, the lowest appropriation for a state convention was $20,000 for Rhode Island's in 1973. (Rhode Island had a tradition of offering its delegates expenses only. After 1960, however, all other states paid convention delegates a salary.)[68] Texas's 1974 convention topped the appropriation's list with $3.8 million.

The next step for a legislature in the preconvention phase is to set a time frame for the assembly. Planners could follow the outline developed by Sturm based on conventions held between 1938 and 1968. He observed that conventions usually fall into three stages: the organizational phase, which consists of seating delegates, adopting rules, electing officers, appointing committees, and attending to other formalities in getting the convention under way, lasting up to two weeks in the major conventions; the committee phase, during which substantive committees receive proposals, hold hearings, make decisions, and draft recommendations for consideration by the whole body; and the ultimate phase of full-scale debate, final decision making, and action on proposals taken by the plenary assembly. Duration of conventions obviously depends on the scope of their individual mandates.[69] The D.C. statehood convention roughly followed Sturm's framework and completed a draft constitution in under five months, which is about average for most state conventions.

One of the less glamorous, yet important, tasks of convention organization is the arrangement of physical facilities. In determining the location of state conventions, planners have considered geographical access, proximity to the state capital, access to proper library facilities, and, obviously, availability of convention facilities and accommodations for delegates and staff. The capital city usually can provide all of these needs, but some state conventions (e.g., New Jersey and Alaska) have met on the campuses of their respective state universities. A well-appointed campus can provide the physical facilities for a convention as well as a scholarly atmosphere removed from the political fray.[70]

Arranging the physical accouterments of a convention may seem mundane, but it plays a crucial role in the smooth operation and morale of the assembly. Delegate Schrag, for instance, reported the frustrations incurred by the D.C. convention when it had to contend with a lack of designated space for committee meetings, no file cabinets for their records, and no recorders of committee meeting minutes. To add to their headaches, the delegates struggled with an obsolete copying machine throughout the entire convention. Such support problems were evident early on, but a limited budget precluded alleviation of the inadequacies.[71]

Adoption of convention rules is another integral step in organizing a convention. Cornwell has issued several caveats for this endeavor. The first is to avoid adoption of the legislature's normal rules, which apply to a different body with different goals from a convention. Second, each convention must draft its own set of rules to meet its own context. Wholesale borrowing of another convention's rules could prove disastrous. At the same time, rules of prior conventions can provide guidance and alert delegates to issues that need early resolution. Third, the rules should provide for expedient handling of convention business while ensuring fair access and full hearings to all interested parties.[72] Thus a honed juggling skill would be the prime talent for a rule drafter and implementor at any convention.

The Rhode Island convention of 1964–69 demonstrated the pitfalls of overly rigid rules. Cornwell writes,

By requiring that every proposal introduced by a delegate must go to a committee and must be reported out and acted on the floor, and by requiring that a public hearing be held on each proposal, the rules committee hoped to insure full delegate and public involvement. The procedures specified, plus the fact some of them were interpreted very rigidly, produced a very cumbersome deliberative process. The delegates found it endlessly repetitious. Thirty-eight percent said "waste of time" as the thing they liked least about being a delegate and 22 percent cited the slow pace of the convention.[73]

Indeed, the five-year Rhode Island assembly was a record breaker in the annals of state constitutional conventions!

The lessons to be learned from committee organization in past conventions are parallel to rules formation. An assembly needs enough to keep the convention running smoothly but not so many as to make the procedure cumbersome. The scope of a convention's mandate would determine the number of substantive committees. Obviously, a convention limited to one topic or even several would not need committees to investigate every article of the existing constitution. But virtually all conventions would find useful the following auxiliary committees: committee on rules, committee on administration, committee on style and drafting, and committee on public information.[74] The last committee would not be as crucial at a national convention as at the state level where constitutional revision is subject to a public referendum. Nevertheless, an informed citizenry would be desirable (if not always attainable) under the Article V procedure.

As noted earlier, the inherent differences between government at the national level and at the state level are reflected in their respective convention procedures. Nevertheless, this chapter identifies the parallels and similarities that do exist between the two amendment processes. Commentators on a potential national convention and certainly planners of such a convocation would miss a valuable store of information if they failed to heed the numerous apposite lessons of state convention precedents.

NOTES

1. Albert L. Sturm and Janice C. May, "State Constitutions and Constitutional Revision: 1968–87," in *The Book of States 1988–89*, Vol. 27 (Lexington, KY: Council of State Governments, 1988), p. 2.

2. Elmer E. Cornwell, Jr., *Constitutional Conventions: The Politics of Revision* (New York: National Municipal League, 1974), p. 13.

3. Sturm and May provide thorough, up-to-date statistics in their annual reports in *The Book of States*; see note 1. supra.

4. Ibid.

5. Cornwell, in *The Constitutional Convention as an Amending Device*, Kermit Hall, Harold M. Hyman, and Leon V. Sigal, eds. (Washington, DC: American Political Science Association and American Historical Association, 1981), p. 11 (original emphasis).

6. Francis H. Heller, "Limiting a Constitutional Convention: The State Precedents," *Cardozo Law Review*, 3 (1982), 564.

7. See Paul J. Weber, "The Constitutional Convention: A Safe Political Option," *The Journal of Law and Politics*, 3 (Winter 1986), 58–64. The questions are adopted from Laurence Tribe's "Issues Raised by Requesting Congress to Call a Constitutional Convention to Propose a Balanced Budget Amendment," *Pacific Law Journal* 10 (1979), 638–640. Russell L. Caplan of the U.S. Department of Justice, whose study of Article V was released just as our book went into production, concludes: "It is far more dangerous to allow a convention drive to progress to its final stages with many critical questions left unanswered than to provide minimal guidance." See *Constitutional Brinkmanship: Amending the Constitution by National Convention* (New York: Oxford University Press, 1988), p. 163.

8. This very helpful table appeared in a Note in the *Harvard Journal of Legislation*, 11 (1973), 145. The parenthetical additions under the "calling" stage include those who may be involved in the selection of delegates to the convention.

9. See Sturm and May's Table 1.4 in their article in the *Book of States*. It lists procedures for calling constitutional conventions in all fifty states.

10. See Chapter 4, supra, for a history of the frustration faced by supporters of movements to call a national convention.

11. Robert J. Martineau, "The Mandatory Referendum on Calling a State Constitutional Convention: Enforcing the People's Right to Reform Their Government," *Ohio State Law Journal* 31, (1970), 422.

12. Sturm and May, pp. 2–3.

13. Martineau, p. 423.

14. Ibid., p. 424.

15. Ibid., p. 426–427.

16. *Chenault V. Carter*, 332 S.W.2d at 626 (Ky. 1960); quoted by Martineau, *The Mandatory Referendum*, p. 430.

17. Ibid.

18. Martineau, p. 431.

19. Ibid., p. 436.

20. 307 U.S. 459.

21. Quoted in Doyle W. Buckwalter, "Constitutional Conventions and State Legislators," *Journal of Public Law*, 20 (1971), 557.

22. Heller, "Limiting a Constitutional Convention," p. 579.

23. Ibid.

24. Ibid., pp. 576–579.

25. Ibid., 577–579.

26. The *Harvard Journal of Legislation* Note arrives at a different conclusion from Heller. The latter refutes the conclusion in the Note by arguing that its author(s) did not appreciate the jurisprudential concept held by state judges that the delegation of the amending power was ineffective unless it was sanctioned by a direct popular vote, p. 578.

27. The basic concept of "sovereignty" denotes "a theory of politics which claims that in every system of government there must be some absolute power of final decision exercised by some person or body recognized both as competent to decide and as able to enforce the decision." The foregoing definition of sovereignty, offered by Bernard Crick, is deceptively simple. Crick has summarized the complex and sometimes murky history of the concept and the variety of interpretations of it as applied to regimes. See his entry in the *International Encyclopedia of the Social Sciences*, Vol. 15, David L. Sills, ed. (New York: Macmillan and the Free Press, 1968), pp. 77–82.

28. As quoted in the *Harvard Journal of Legislation*, p. 146.

29. *Harvard Journal of Legislation*, p. 147 (original emphasis).

30. Ibid.

31. Ibid., p. 148.

32. John Alexander Jameson, *A Treatise on the Constitutional Convention: Its History, Powers, and Modes of Proceeding*, 2d ed. (Chicago: E.B. Myers, 1869), p. 64.

33. Thomas A. Gilliam, "Constitutional Conventions: Precedents, Problems, and Proposals," *St. Louis University Law Journal* (1971).

34. Jameson, *A Treatise on the Constitutional Convention*, p. 351.

35. *Quinlan v. Houston & T.C. Ry*, 89 Tex 356, 376, 34 S.W. 738, 744 (1896); as quoted in the *Harvard Journal of Legislation*, p. 129.

36. See this chapter, infra, for a discussion of instances of the use of limited conventions at the state level.

37. As quoted by Wilber S. Legg, "Can Public Officials Be Delegates to the Constitutional Convention?" *Chicago Bar Record* (1968).

38. Ibid.

39. Of course, such a view may conflict with the concept of a limit-

able convention. If a constitutional convention is equal to and independent of the other branches of government, could it be limited by
those branches?

40. U.S. Congress, Senate Committee on the Judiciary, *Constitutional
Convention Procedures, Hearing before the Subcommittee on the Constitution
on S. 3, S. 520, and S. 1710.* 96th Cong., 1st sess., 1979, p. 43.

41. As quoted in Cornwell, *The Constitutional Convention*, p. 33.

42. All of the above quotations appear in Cornwell, pp. 33–34.

43. Philip G. Schrag, *Behind the Scenes: The Politics of a Constitutional
Convention* (Washington, DC: Georgetown University Press, 1985), p. 41.
Schrag's book offers an engaging and enlightening look at the political
machinations of a constitutional convention.

44. Ibid., pp. 42–43. In a revealing incident, one of the authors,
testifying before a committee of the Michigan legislature, noted that
people elected to conventions are strikingly similar to people elected
to state legislatures. One legislator interrupted to say "that may be of
great comfort to you, Professor, but it scares the hell out of me!"

45. Cornwell, *The Constitutional Convention*, pp. 34–35.

46. Jameson, *A Treatise on the Constitutional Convention*, p. 255.

47. *The Constitutional Convention: A Manual on Its Planning, Organization and Operation*, prepared by John P. Wheeler, Jr. (New York:
National Municipal League, 1961), pp. 30–31.

48. Albert L. Sturm, *Thirty Years of State Constitution-Making: 1938–
68* (New York: National Municipal League, 1970), p. 69.

49. Wheeler, *The Constitutional Convention*, pp. 32–33.

50. Ibid., p. 33.

51. American Bar Association Special Constitutional Convention
Study Committee, *Amendment of the Constitution by the Convention Method
Under Article V* (Chicago: ABA, 1974).

52. Peter A. Tomei, "Con Con at the Crossroads: Convention of the
Parties or of the People?" *Chicago Bar Record*, December 1968. Tomei
provides a detailed account of the history of partisanship in state constitutional conventions.

53. Ibid.

54. Ibid.

55. Ibid.

56. See p. 92., supra, and Tomei, who argues that Maryland's difficulties may also be traced to submitting the entire product of the
convention to the electorate at one time. Breaking the constitution down
into more manageable parts may have been a better strategy for the
reformers. Moreover, the new constitution's proponents failed to mount
a grassroots campaign for ratification. Finally, the social unrest of the

late 1960s created an environment among the electorate that was wary, if not hostile, to change. Thus the lack of success of the Maryland convention was traceable to factors beyond its nonpartisan make-up.

57. Jameson, *A Treatise on the Constitutional Convention*, p. 264.

58. Ibid.

59. *Goodrich v. Moore*, 2 Minn. 61, 66 (1858). As quoted in the *Harvard Journal of Legislation*, Note, 133.

60. Ibid. Other leading cases that support the point indirectly include *Carton v. Secretary of State*, 151 Mich. 337, 340, 115 N.W. 429 (1908); also see Roger S. Hoar, *Constitutional Conventions: Their Nature, Powers, and Limitations* (Boston: Little, Brown, 1917), Chapter IX, for a discussion of unsuccessful attempts at legislative control of state conventions.

61. *Harvard Journal of Legislation*, Note, 134.

62. Sturm, *Thirty Years of State Constitution-Making*, pp. 62–66, especially Table 12 on pp. 65–66.

63. See Council of State Governments, *Book of States*, 1972–88.

64. See Hoar, *Constitutional Conventions*, pp. 111–115. Examples of limited conventions that overrode limitations are those in Georgia (1789), Minnesota (1857), Pennsylvania (1872), Alabama (1901), Virginia (1901), and Michigan (1908).

65. Richard J. Conners concluded that these were among the lessons to be learned from the New Jersey convention experience in the 1940s. See his *The Process of Constitutional Revision in New Jersey: 1940–1947* (New York: National Municipal League, 1970).

66. Schrag, *Behind the Scenes*, pp. 64–65.

67. See Council of States, *Book of States*, 1972–1988, for lists of state appropriations for conventions.

68. Sturm, *Thirty Years of State Constitution-Making*, p. 70.

69. Ibid., pp. 74–76.

70. Wheeler, *The Constitutional Convention*, p. 8.

71. Schrag, *Behind the Scenes*, p. 134.

72. Cornwell, *The Constitutional Convention*, p. 55.

73. Ibid.

74. Wheeler, *The Constitutional Convention*, pp. 42–48. Wheeler's constitutional convention manual is a helpful source for convention planners interested in a step-by-step approach to organizing an assembly.

6

THE CONSTITUTIONAL CONVENTION: A SAFE POLITICAL OPTION

CONTEMPORARY DISCUSSIONS OF constitutional conventions generally take place on two levels: in academic or scholarly literature and in the popular media. Rarely do these different discussions affect each other. There is, however, one exception: the issue of the "safety" of a constitutional convention. Unfortunately, many scholars have done the nation a disservice by concocting hypothetical horribles.[1] They focus on whether a constitutional convention would jeopardize civil liberties or produce a constitutional, economic, or social crisis. These hypothetical problems are then magnified by the media, distracting public attention from the real problems addressed by those who call for a convention.[2]

This chapter explores the various points in the constitutional convention amendment procedure whereby political "safety latches" would prevent a convention from becoming the Pandora's box that some commentators fear. It describes the forces that protect the democratic process and concludes that amending the federal Constitution by means of a convention would be a safe political procedure for the nation to pursue. In this context, "safe" means that the procedure allows input into the amending process by a variety of political forces at various points and over an extended period of time such that a consensus within the nation is reached; that procedures are established to resolve potential impasses in the process; and that the process retains the aura of legitimacy necessary for political stability and voluntary compliance with the law. In short, the convention procedure protects the nation from either a coup d'état or a breakdown in the political process. It is a democratic remedy for problems in a democratic society.

METHODOLOGY OF THE ANALYSIS

Those who argue that a constitutional convention is risky assume that unsettled law is unsafe law. But that assumption is true only if the people, procedures, and precedents already authorized to settle law are unwilling or unable to function. Such is not the case within the framework of the American political structure.

Discussions limited to the legality of the process of calling and conducting a convention are sterile, for they fail to consider the political aspect of a convention. This failure to consider political reality is exemplified by three substantially different questions about constitutional conventions, which are best addressed separately. What *could* a convention do? What *should* a convention do? What *would* a convention do?

The first question is most properly within the domain of the constitutional lawyer; the second, within the domain of the normative theoretician from one of several academic disciplines (including law and political science); and the third, most properly within the domain of the political scientist.[3] What a convention would do involves predicting what political actors will do. Such a prediction is based on empirically verified historical and contemporary evidence and will be itself eventually verifiable.

The literature on constitutional conventions is dominated by legal academicians, with contributions by a smattering of historians and, rarely, a political scientist. Lawyers and those who "think like lawyers" argue from a legal perspective: that is, either in a deductive mode from general principles to specific certainties or by analogy from relevant precedents.[4]

Deduction is a valid and valuable mode of argumentation because it develops the steps and explores the gaps in an argument. It can show, for example, what specific actions are required for Congress to call and conduct a constitutional convention.

Deductive analysis also explores what Professor Laurence Tribe referred to as an unanswered and unanswerable question raised by Article V.[5] The article's text does not address the format and timing of applications and does not specify what would constitute valid applications from two-thirds of the states. The issue of whether a state may rescind its call for a convention is never addressed, nor is the issue of whether Congress may call a convention for a limited purpose.

If one seeks legally certain answers to those questions through deduction from the text of Article V, Professor Tribe is correct in characterizing them as unanswerable. Nor are the standard tools of constitutional interpretation helpful. A "plain meaning" analysis can lead to some interesting conclusions, but not to certainty. The intent of the Framers is only slightly less obscure; unfortunately, despite their brilliance, the Framers simply did not address many of our present concerns. Most certainly, they did not provide procedures for the call and conduct of constitutional conventions.

Precedents established by the courts, although more useful than simple deduction, nevertheless cannot provide certainty. The meaning and requirements of Article V are not thoroughly litigated areas of the law, and the courts' interpretations are inconsistent. Without authoritative precedents, lawyers face the uncomfortable prospect of relying on a few questionable decisions such as *Coleman v. Miller*.[6] Consequently, their analyses are developed through logical reasoning, by analogy to the existing precedents, and by reliance on the academic literature.

Academics focus on the potential problems inherent in the convention process and offer possible solutions. Their articles discuss what could or could not be done within the constitutional framework and what the states, Congress, or the courts should or should not do. Such discourse performs a valuable service. In this ample literature, the ramifications and implications of any interpretation can be drawn out before a real case arises and requires a real decision.[7]

The most useful tool for analyzing the issue of the *safety* of a constitutional convention is political inference.[8] It is a method of induction, which moves from patterns of specific observations to general conclusions. It is based on the systematic accumulation of evidence drawn from political and social experiences. Although it recognizes that absolute certainty in the realm of human affairs is unobtainable, political inference nevertheless can be a reliable method of predicting future events.

A number of well-accepted political inferences are relevant to the present discussion. For example, barring cataclysmic events, the political culture and values of a society are stable over time and change only slightly. The behavior of most citizens and most institutions in a stable society is highly predictable, even in times of stress and change, and whenever possible, citizens and institutions will handle new problems by following patterns they established to handle old problems. In the United States, mass voting patterns and political ideologies are relatively stable over time. Political elites rarely reject the political values or destroy the political and social institutions within which they rose to success.

When established political institutions function within what the public perceives to be their normal parameters, they retain their legitimacy, whereas new institutions strive to function as much as possible in traditional patterns in order to establish their legitimacy. New issues are either added to the political agenda when established elites see them as a significant means to retain or regain political power, or added by nonelites (e.g., through popular referenda) only to be co-opted by established elites. No established political groups or elites will stand aside and allow their power bases to be reduced or destroyed without attempting to defend against such attacks.

These insights arise from observations of political behavior. They provide a means to plot what will happen at each stage in the process of calling and convening a constitutional convention. They are based on both vertical (meaning historically, over several decades) and horizontal (meaning including a variety of political actors, issues, and events) factors. Of course, the validity of predictions made through political inference, as with other inferences, depends on the amount of evidence or experience from which the inference is drawn. Here, however, there are important differences between the legal and political inquiries. From a legal perspective, no amount of empirical evidence will allow us to draw conclusions of legal certainty. The question, however, is not whether the results of any process are uncertain, but whether the results of action are less risky than the results of not acting. As one author has observed, "We must act in the courage of our uncertainties."[9]

From a political perspective, however, we can make political inferences that demonstrate that a constitutional convention would be an extraordinarily safe political procedure.

ANALYSIS: THE SAFETY MEASURES WITHIN ARTICLE V

The Two-thirds Requirement

As is obvious from the text of Article V, the first safety valve is the application for a constitutional convention by two-thirds of the state legislatures. Scholars and editors may impugn the wisdom, integrity, or motivation of state legislators, but those legislators are an enormous hurdle for all who propose a convention. As noted earlier, since 1789 there have been more than 400 calls for a convention, including at least one from every state. *Not one* has succeeded in clearing the two-thirds barrier.[10]

At the very least, this indicates a conviction that not every subject ought to be addressed in constitutional terms. The state legislators have recognized that not every societal problem requires a constitutional solution, and where a constitutional solution is required, amendments proposed by Congress are preferred to those proposed by the states. Undoubtedly some calls in some states are made irresponsibly, but there is convincing empirical evidence that as applications near the required majority, state legislatures treat the matter seriously, with what might be called a "fourth-quarter cautiousness."[11] This record indicates that the constitutional requirement that state legislatures in two-thirds of the states make applications to Congress for a convention operates as an important check on rash, divisive, unwise, or unnecessary amendments as well as a hurdle for those that are wise and necessary.

Clearing the state legislature hurdle is even more formidable than the text of Article V indicates. Since all the states but Nebraska have bicameral legislatures, and both houses of those state legislatures must pass a convention call, a majority of *one* house in each of seventeen states could defeat a call.

As a critical point approaches, the media begin alerting the public, interest groups organize their campaigns, governors apply pressure, and political elites take sides. In short, politics takes over. Arguments over the issue and the process are made, including the familiar contention that constitutional conventions are the Pandora's box of American politics.

Even Congress becomes interested when the numbers close in. On at least four occasions, the almost-certain call for a convention prompted Congress to propose amendments on its own.[12] Indeed, forcing Congress to act is arguably one purpose of current applications for a convention.[13] Faced with the inevitable, members of Congress are quite likely to act simply to avoid the inconvenience and expense of a convention, as well as to avoid the appearance of impotence.

Calling the Convention

Although calling a convention is clearly the prerogative and obligation of Congress, it has never exercised that power, and discussions of the possible problems are purely theoretical. Questions abound about two parts of the convention process: first, the application for a convention, and, second, the procedures Congress may establish for the election of delegates and for the convention itself. Questions about the application process include what constitutes a valid application, who determines validity, and what happens if Congress refuses to act. Questions about convention procedures ask whether Congress can limit a convention to one topic, whether it can limit the time for deliberation, who determines the qualifications of delegates, and what happens when convention delegates ignore the rules and conditions set by Congress.

The answers to these questions could significantly affect the distribution of power within a convention. Thus it is reasonable to expect that they will be the object of considerable politicking during a call for a convention. Legislators opposed to the *content* of a proposed amendment will use various delaying tactics, including challenges to the validity of applications. Interest groups, the president, scholars, and voters will exert whatever influence they can muster. In addition, many important questions will continue to be debated by serious scholars.[14]

Nonetheless, the instruments for resolving any conflicts among these groups are already established and are capable of settling the disputes. The first mechanism is Congress itself. Beginning in 1967 with a bill drafted by Senator Sam J. Ervin of North Carolina, the Senate has passed a series of bills establishing procedures should a convention be called. One bill, S.40, unanimously approved by the Senate Judiciary Committee on September 10, 1985, did not pass the Senate.[15] The corresponding inability of the House to pass any of the proposed bills further exemplifies the intense political pressures produced by debate about the possibility of a constitutional convention. Although Congress has thus failed to establish convention procedures, the introduction and passage in the Senate of these bills demonstrates that it could do so if faced with the prospect of a convention.

The second mechanism for resolving disputes is the Supreme Court. The proper role of the Court in Article V disputes is a hotly contested issue. Walter E. Dellinger set out a persuasive argument for a judicial role, which answers most objections:

[S]uch review is justified as an initial matter by the same considerations that have made judicial review an accepted part of the constitutional system since *Marbury v. Madison*. The Constitution is positive law—law that may be invoked in court by litigants. In fulfilling its role as a resolver of legal disputes, a court must interpret and apply all of the law applicable to the cases before it, including the law of the Constitution. The provisions of Article V are fully a part of that law.[16]

The thesis of Dellinger's argument is that *Coleman v. Miller*, a decision excluding the courts from Article V litigation, was wrongly decided.[17] *Coleman* declared the amending process to be " 'political' in its entirety, from the submission of an amendment until it becomes part of the Constitution, and therefore not subject to judicial guidance, control, or interference at any point."[18] Dellinger concluded that *Coleman* should be overturned.

One may go further and argue that eventually *Coleman* will be overturned not only because it was wrongly decided the first time, but because the political question doctrine has been radically transformed since 1939.[19] The Court has demonstrated its willingness to limit what it considers strictly political in *Reynolds v. Sims*[20] and *Baker v. Carr*,[21] and cases as diverse as *Roe v. Wade*[22] and *Brown v. Hartlage*[23] indicate that the Court will step in to decide problems it deems unresolvable in the political arena.

To argue that the Court *should* keep its hands off the amendment process is quite different from saying that the Court's hands are tied. Clearly, they are not. It is a legitimate legal question to ask what the courts *should* do, but the raw political question is what the courts *will* do. The history of our judicial system bears witness to the fact that the courts will not allow an unresolved legal dispute to become an unresolvable political dispute.

In brief, although there are unsettled legal questions about calling a convention, there are also institutions capable of settling them in a legitimate manner.

Election of Delegates

The selection of delegates for a convention is one of the most critical, yet unexamined, phases of the process. In testimony before a California State Assembly committee, Professor Tribe listed a number of unanswered questions about the selection and function of delegates:[24]

—Who would be eligible to serve as a delegate?

—Must delegates be specially elected? Could Congress simply appoint its own members?

—Are the states to be equally represented, or must the one-person, one-vote rule apply?

—Would delegates be committed to cast a vote one way or the other on a proposed amendment?

—Would delegates at a convention enjoy immunity parallel to that of members of Congress?

—Are delegates to be paid? If so, by whom?

—Could delegates be recalled? Could the convention expel delegates? On what grounds?

Tribe implied that these questions are unanswerable. In fact, the original Ervin bill did answer these questions. The subsequent S.40 provides answers for nearly all of them, although it does not address Tribe's somewhat specious question as to whether an elected delegate would be committed to vote as he or she had pledged on a proposed amendment.[25] The rules set forth in S.40 are not perfect, but they are workable. Legal challenges will certainly be raised by those with a stake in keeping such questions unanswered, but when the legislature fails, the court system provides an established, institutionalized procedure for resolving such disputes.

Another intriguing question concerns who would run for a post as delegate. Assuming that Congress will set requirements such as those proposed in S.40, that "[elections] will be held in each state in the manner provided by state law [, and] no Senator or Representative, or person holding an office of trust or profit under the United States shall be elected as delegate," experience with past elections should suggest who would be likely to run.

Thus we can anticipate that the pool of delegates will include those who have an active interest in the purpose of the convention and who are willing to take a position for or against amendments; who like the public spotlight and whose personal affairs can withstand public scrutiny; who have name recognition (and therefore a chance of winning in a relatively short campaign period); who have financial and organizational support; and who have some experience in waging campaigns and can devote time to campaigning.[26] Although there will certainly be a variety of candidates who do not fit these characteristics, they are, as shown below, very unlikely to win many seats. These five characteristics suggest that politicians and other prominent people who have succeeded in the current system, as well as people backed by political parties and financed by established interests, are likely to become the delegates.

Common sense and past experience suggest there will be active participation by political parties, interest groups, local and national media, and influential public figures in the delegate election campaigns.[27] Candidates will be asked repeatedly about their positions on proposed amendments, forcing them to answer directly or to hedge. They also will be asked many other questions, including whether they will abide by the rules established by Congress, whether they will consider amendments other than the one for which the convention was called, and whether they will touch the Bill of Rights.

Since candidates will be asked and forced to answer the "confrontational" and "runaway" questions *before* they are elected, a logical assumption is that they will take positions that are in accordance with their personal beliefs on the substantive issues *and* that are most likely to enhance their chances of being elected on the procedural issues. Except for instances of the collapse of societal infrastructures (e.g., in times of war or famine) those who are elected are those who take safe, or centrist, positions on procedural questions.[28] At the very least, voters will know how candidates stand on the critical questions and cast their votes accordingly.[29]

Although it is foolish to attempt to predict who will win elections before candidates are chosen or issues raised, a few general conclusions can be drawn. American voters are distributed across the political ideological spectrum in a roughly bell-shaped curve. That is, those voters with "extreme" or "radical" views tend to be strong in conviction but few in number and represent the left and right extremes of the curve. Those with progressively more moderate views make up in numerical strength what they lack in intensity of conviction.

Anyone who wishes to win an election in a system where voters' views are distributed in a bell curve must either convince large numbers of people to change their political views or appeal to the more moderate among the electorate. Given the short time in which a campaign would be waged, and the difficulty of modifying political convictions, winning candidates will be those who can appeal to the largest number of moderate voters. Obviously, in some cases moderates will favor the substance of proposed amendment and in some cases will oppose it. If the proposed amendment is itself a radical departure from current practice, the moderates will be quite difficult to persuade.

Once the veil is removed from the process of selecting the delegates, the results look stunningly familiar. Candidates are chosen, campaigns are run, and elections are won in a process that involves numerous, seasoned actors functioning in predictable patterns through established institutions. People who are elected as delegates will overwhelmingly represent the mainstreams of their electoral districts. They will be people who have succeeded in the existing political environment and who are highly unlikely to approve radical changes. This predictability of the actors and their actions provides yet another significant safeguard in the process of amending the Constitution via the convention route.

THE CONVENTION AND RATIFICATION PROCESS

One gets the impression from the literature that a constitutional convention is like the mystical beast of the apocalypse—once loosed it can never be caged. Alarmists claim that impairment of the constitutional protections and structure will begin with the convention. Senator John Stennis of Mississippi summed up the fears of many: "[W]hat is there to insure that the convention would not become a runaway assembly which would try to rewrite our basic law in numerous particulars? There are too many unanswered and unanswerable legal questions and problems involved to make the convention procedure worthy of the risk involved."[30]

The core of this fear is that there are too many unsettled legal questions for a convention to be safe. Questions follow four themes.

First, can Congress set rules for the convention? If so, must the convention follow them? What happens if it doesn't?

Second, can a convention be called for a limited purpose, i.e., to approve a single amendment, or is amending power unlimited?

Third, if it can be called to consider a specific amendment, must delegates simply vote yea or nay, or may they compromise, amend, or change the text?

Fourth, who controls matters such as the pay of delegates, length of the convention session, and number of voters needed to pass an amendment?

Legal scholars have provided a variety of answers to these questions—not all of which are disinterested. Those who have a stake in making a convention appear unpalatable attempt to create an aura of mystery and suggest that a convention would be unpredictable. Yet when the convention process is examined in the light of political experience, much of this mystery and uncertainty disappears.

It is clear that Congress can set rules for the convention, since Article V lacks explicit language to the contrary. S.40 establishes a number of applicable rules and if it or a similar bill were to pass, that would provide statutory law governing conventions. The question then is whether the Supreme Court would uphold such a statute. Certainly, the subject matter falls reasonably within the principle of implied powers established in *McCulloch v. Maryland*: "Any means which tend directly to the execution of the constitutional powers of the government are in themselves constitutional."[31] But even if the Court in a particular situation declined to uphold congressional power to set rules, it has at least answered the question of whether Congress is allowed to set rules.

More critical are concerns about what would happen in the convention and what is to ensure that it will not become a runaway convention. Opponents focus on the lack of *legal* constraints. In a classic statement cited by Professor Tribe, Senator Weldon Heyburn of Idaho made a veiled allusion to the ominous notion of sovereignty:

When the people of the United States meet in a constitutional convention there is no power to limit their action. They are greater than the Constitution, and they can repeal the provision that limits the right of amendment. They can repeal every section of it, because they are the peers of the people who made it.[32]

To underscore this point, Tribe asks, "Was Senator Heyburn right or wrong? If right, then a constitutional convention could propose any imaginable amendment, no matter how limited the official scope of the convention. Although *opinions* contrary to the Senator's may be found, the undeniable fact is that *no definitive answer exists*."[33] Tribe is correct, of course, in the same sense that there is no truly definitive answer to any question about future events.

What Professor Tribe ignores are the *political* constraints that ensure that no convention is likely to get out of control. There are a number of such constraints: the previously cited character of the delegates elected; the media attention that will be given to discrepancies between the campaign statements and promises and the delegates' actual words and actions; the number of delegates and divisions within the convention itself, which would make it extraordinarily difficult for one faction or a radical position to prevail; the delegates' awareness that the convention results must be presented to Congress, which might not forward any amendment that went beyond the convention mandate; the Supreme Court, which might well declare certain actions beyond the constitutional powers of the convention; and most important of all, the need to get the proposed amendment ratified not only by the thirty-four states that called for the convention, but by thirty-eight states.

More effective constraints on a constitutional convention can hardly be imagined. Although this analysis does not answer all the questions about what could or would happen in a convention, it does point out the political constraints that provide protection against a runaway or "unsafe" convention. It also illustrates that the process and institutions necessary for answering the questions are well established and quite capable of functioning when the occasions arise.[34]

Another safety provision is found in the procedure following the convention. When the delegates finish their work, their proposed amendments are forwarded to Congress for distribution to state legislatures or conventions in each state as determined by Congress. Since this has never actually occurred, there are a number of unresolved legal questions.

To what degree may Congress—under its Article V power to propose a "Mode of Ratification" or ancillary to its Article V power to "call a Convention" or pursuant to its Article I power under the Necessary and Proper clause—either refuse to submit to the states a proposed amendment for ratification or decide to submit such an amendment under a severe limit? What if Congress and the Convention disagree on these matters?[35]

But these theoretical questions ignore reality since, when questions arise in an actual convention, institutions and processes will have been established to answer them. Congress itself could provide most of the answers beforehand by enacting a bill similar to S.40.[36] And in cases of disagreement between Congress and the convention, the Supreme Court could also provide definitive answers.

Political forces that often limit congressional discretion will also affect the potential ratification of the proposed amendment. Opponents of the amendment can be expected to claim that the convention went beyond its mandate and the amendments ought not to be forwarded, or to delay the forwarding by a filibuster and other parliamentary maneuvers.[37] Certainly, political strategists would plot which of the two modes of ratification would most likely lead to the success or failure of the amendment and would use that procedure to attempt to reach their policy objective. Whether Congress forwards the convention resolution, delays it unreasonably, or forwards it with its own recommendations, legal challenges can be expected. Once amendments are passed by a convention and forwarded to the states for ratification, they will be subjected to intensive media coverage and minute analysis from interest groups and other affected parties. Attempting to personalize and dramatize the historical event, reporters will probe the intentions and motivations of convention delegates, highlight the conflicts and compromises, and evaluate the results.

The president will also most likely become involved if the amendment affects presidential prerogatives or powers. Although there is some discussion about the formal role of a president in the amending process, there is little question that presidents may use their immense informal powers to influence Congress and the public at large.

Finally, as the Equal Rights Amendment struggle has shown, the most critical stage is not proposing, but ratifying, an amendment. At the ratification stage the requisite number is increased by four states to thirty-eight, making ratification of amendments more difficult than proposing them.[38] A significant difference at the ratification stage is that political maneuvering will take place in fifty different arenas, each well established, perceived as legitimate and accustomed to political pressures, and fully capable of acting independently of the other state arenas.

Additional difficulties will doubtless arise, since during the time it takes to call and conduct a convention, interest groups at all levels will have organized and determined their strategies. An immense amount of analysis, public debate, and politicking also will occur long before any amendment is submitted to the states for ratification. This informal political process provides an enormous obstacle to unpopular, hasty, ill-conceived, or unwise constitutional amendments.

CONCLUSION

The original Constitution was not only a legal document; it was also a political document. It set out not simply legal principles, but legal principles hammered out of political compromise and anchored in political realism. The primary safeguards of democracy envisioned by the Framers were political, not legal. Nowhere is this more evident than in the procedures set forth to amend the Constitution by means of a convention. History has not only borne testimony to the wisdom of the Framers, but has provided evidence to reinforce their trust in the political process. Is the constitutional convention process safe? It requires a consensus of at least 75 percent of the state legislatures or assemblies in addition to the active cooperation of Congress and the courts, and at least some established political elites and interest groups to pass an amendment by this means. It is a procedure that requires so much time that short-term passions or temporary coalitions could not prevail.

There are surely more serious dangers to the nation's liberties than a constitutional convention. Notwithstanding the arguments of legal scholars with limited methodological tools (or partisan objectives) and political columnists with active imaginations, calling a constitutional convention would be a safe political process. As James Madison observed in *Federalist* No. 51: "In the extended republic of the United States and among the great variety of interests, parties and sects which it embraces, a coalition of a majority of the whole society could seldom take place on any other principles than those of justice and the general good."[39]

NOTES

1. See, Arthur Goldberg, "The Proposed Constitutional Convention," *Hastings Constitutional Law Quarterly* 11 (1983); see also Gerald Gunther, "Constitutional Roulette: The Dimensions of the Risk," in *The Constitution and the Budget*, W. S. Moore and Rudolph Penner, eds. (Washington, DC: American Enterprise Institute for Public Policy Research, 1980), p. 5.

2. This chapter takes no position on the value, wisdom, or merits of specific amendments that are the bases of calls for a convention, but Chapter 7, infra, will evaluate the wisdom of the balanced budget amendment.

3. This is not to be taken in the "turf-tending" sense; rather it emphasizes that the methodologies used in particular disciplines are more applicable to different types of questions.

4. Benjamin N. Cardozo, *The Nature of the Judicial Process* (New Haven: Yale University Press, 1921).

5. Tribe, "Issues Raised by Requesting Congress to Call a Constitutional Convention to Propose a Balanced Budget Amendment," *Pacific Law Journal* 10 (1979), 627. Professor Tribe has moved beyond the rhetoric of runaway conventions and refers to the "risks" of possible confrontations: (1) between Congress and the convention, (2) between Congress and the Supreme Court, and (3) between the Supreme Court and the states. Initially, this approach appears both innovative and more plausible than the more traditional argument about the possibility of a "runaway" convention. But it suffers the same defect—it totally ignores the political process and looks for certainty in settled law rather than in the safety of established political procedures. Undoubtedly, confrontations will occur just as they regularly do between the branches of government. Each time the Supreme Court declares an act of Congress or of a state unconstitutional, it risks a con-

frontation. Such confrontations are followed by acquiescence, accommodation, or compromise. The same will occur with a constitutional convention.

6. 307 U.S. 433 (1939). According to the Court in *Baker v. Carr*, 369 U.S. 186 (1962), *Coleman* supports the proposition that "questions of how long a proposed amendment to the Federal Constitution remained open to ratification, and what effect a prior rejection had on a subsequent ratification, were committed to congressional resolution and involved criteria of decision that necessarily escaped judicial grasp." See also *United States v. Sprague*, 282 U.S. 716 (1931); *Leser v. Garnet*, 258 U.S. 130 (1922); *Dillon v. Gloss*, 256 U.S. 368 (1921); see, generally, Walter Dellinger, "The Legitimacy of Constitutional Change: Rethinking the Amendment Process," *Harvard Law Review* 97 (1983), 386 (critiquing of *Coleman v. Miller*).

7. See, e.g., Walter E. Dellinger, "Constitutional Politics: A Rejoinder," *Harvard Law Review*, 97 (1983), 466; Dellinger, "The Recurring Question of the 'Limited' Constitutional Convention," *Yale Law Journal*, 88 (1979), 1623 (concluding that the states and Congress cannot limit a federal constitutional convention in advance to the consideration of only one issue); Dellinger, "The Legitimacy of Constitutional Change: Rethinking the Amendment Process," *Harvard Law Review*, 97 (1983), 386; Jefferson B. Fordham, "Some Observations Upon Uneasy American Federalism," *North Carolina Law Review*, 58 (1980), 289 (a provocative analysis of the possible content and ramifications of a Federal constitutional convention); Gerald Gunther, "Constitutional Brinkmanship: Stumbling Toward a Convention," *American Bar Association Journal*, 65 (1979), 1046 (state legislatures are calling for a constitutional convention without comprehending the full dimensions of the risks); Francis H. Heller, "Limiting a Constitutional Convention: The State Precedents," *Cardozo Law Review*, 3 (1982) 563 (concluding that state court precedents cannot be used to resolve the question of whether a federal constitutional convention may be limited by the states which apply for it); Philip G. Schrag, "By the People: The Political Dynamics of a Constitutional Convention," *Georgetown Law Journal*, 72 (1984), 819; Laurence Tribe, "A Constitution We are Amending: In Defense of a Restrained Judicial Role," *Harvard Law Review*, 97 (1983), 433; Tribe, "Issues Raised by Requesting Congress to Call a Constitutional Convention to Propose a Balanced Budget Amendment," *Pacific Law Journal*, 10 (1979), 627; Volger, "Amending the Constitution by the Article V Convention Method," *Notre Dame Law Review*, 55 (1979), 355.

8. The concept of political inference is grounded in David Hume,

"Enquiries Concerning Human Understanding and Concerning the Principles of Morals," Sec. VIII, Part 1: "Above one half of human reasonings contain inferences . . . attended with more or less degrees of certainty proportioned to our experience of the usual conduct of mankind in such particular situations."

The classic work on public opinion distribution and stability is V. O. Key, Jr., *Public Opinion and American Democracy* (New York: Knopf, 1961). On opinion and behavior, see Bernard C. Hennessy, *Public Opinion*, 2d ed. (Belmont, CA: Wadsworth publishing, 1970). For a fascinating discussion of the politics of a contemporary state constitutional convention, which also supports the central thesis of this article, see Comparative State Politics Newsletter, 5, No. 4 (August 1984), 4–7. On the rationality of voters, see Anthony Downs, *An Economic Theory of Democracy* (Boston: Little, Brown, 1957). For a succinct, yet comprehensive survey of theoretical styles of contemporary political science, see James G. Marsh and John P. Olson, "The New Institutionalism: Organizational Factors in Political Life," *American Political Science Review*, 78 (1984), 734.

9. Richard J. Neuhaus, *The Naked Public Square* (Grand Rapids: Eerdmans Publishing, 1984), p. 11.

10. American Bar Association, Special Constitutional Convention Study Committee, *Amendment of the Constitution by the Convention Method Under Article V* (Chicago: American Bar Association, p. 60). The A.B.A. reports 356 recorded calls as of 1974. Since that time thirty-two states have called for a convention to balance the budget and nineteen have called for one to propose a human life amendment; see Table 4.1, supra.

11. Linda Healy, "Past and Present Convention Calls: From Gay Abandon to Cautious Resistance," paper presented at Southern Political Science Association meeting Savannah, GA, November 1, 1984.

12. Edward Corwin and Mary L. Ramsey, "The Constitutional Law of Constitutional Amendment," *Notre Dame Law Review*, 26 (1951), 185, 196.

13. See, generally, ibid.

14. See supra note 7.

15. Senate Rep. No. 99–135, 99th Cong., 1st Sess. Constitutional Convention Implementation Act.

16. Walter Dellinger, "The Legitimacy of Constitutional Change: Rethinking the Amendment Process," *Harvard Law Review*, 97 (1984), 411–412 (footnotes omitted); contra, Laurence Tribe, "A Constitution We Are Amending: In Defense of a Restrained Judicial Role," *Harvard Law Review*, 97 (1984), 433.

17. Dellinger, supra note 16.

18. 307 U.S. at 459.

19. The "political question" doctrine posits that some constitutional questions are not subject to judicial review because the final decision-making competency over the issue is within the constitutional authority of another branch of government. Lee A. Albert, "Justiciability and Theories of Judicial Review: A Remote Relationship," *Southern California Law Review*, 50 (1977), 1139, 1161. See Louis Henkin, "Is There a Political Question Doctrine?" *Yale Law Journal*, 86 (1976) 597. (Political question doctrine saw its heyday in the New Deal Court and received its highest measure of devotion from Justice Felix Frankfurter and perhaps its boldest articulation by Justice Hugo Black in *Coleman v. Miller*.)

20. 377 U.S. 533 (1964).

21. 369 U.S. 186 (1962).

22. 410 U.S. 113 (1973).

23. 456 U.S. 45 (1982).

24. Tribe, supra note 5, at 638–639.

25. S.40, 99th Cong., 1st Sess., Sect. 135 (1985); see note 36 infra.

26. C. f. Austin Ranney, "Candidate Selection" in *Democracy at the Polls*, David Butler, et al., eds. (Washington, DC: American Enterprise Institute, 1981), pp. 75–106; Samuel J. Eldersveld, *Political Parties in American Society* (New York: Basic Books, 1982), pp. 195–230, 269–325.

27. Discussions on the role that interest groups play in American politics in general or on the role they are playing in the attempt to call a convention for proposing a balanced budget amendment are missing from the legal literature. For a general discussion of interest group politics, see Jeffrey R. Berry, *The Interest Group Society* (Boston: Little, Brown, 1984); Shirley Elder and Norman Ornstein, *Interest Groups, Lobbying and Policymaking* (Washington, DC: Congressional Quarterly Press, 1978); Mancur Olson Jr., *The Logic of Collective Action* (Cambridge: Harvard University Press, 1965); Robert Salisbury, ed., *Interest Group Politics in America*, (New York: Harper Row, 1970).

A list of speakers before a Senate committee hearings of the Michigan legislature on March 13, 1985, illustrates the involvement of interest groups. Among the speakers were representatives of the Chamber of Commerce, National Tax Limitation Committee, Common Cause, Michigan Manufacturing Association, Coalition of Retiree Groups in Kalamazoo, American Civil Liberties Union, B'nai B'rith, Michigan Association of School Boards, Jewish Community Council of Metro Detroit, and Michigan Association of Realtors. Of these, four favored a balanced budget amendment and seven opposed it. In a joint hearing of the Connecticut House and Senate on March 18, 1985, a similar range of groups was represented with the addition of National Organization of Women, the AFL-CIO, and National Association of Realtors.

One objection to calling a convention is the fear the "special interests" would dominate the process. However, there is nothing in the amending process that would give interest groups more influence than they have in the regular political process. In fact, because a convention would be a novel political event of rather short duration, it is reasonable to expect substantial media coverage, which would publicize interest group efforts to influence the delegates.

28. See, generally, Donald E. Stokes, "What Decided Elections," in *Democracy at the Polls* (1981), pp. 264–292; Theodore Lowi, "Toward Functionalism in Political Science: The Case of Innovation in Party Systems," *American Political Science Review*, 57 (1963), 570.

29. One could hypothesize that candidates would simply lie about their intentions or later change their minds. Given the profiles of the candidates who would run, it is inconceivable that even a substantial minority of the 535 candidates would lie to such an extent. After all, the product of the convention must come again before the states and the delegates must return home.

30. William Edel, *A Constitutional Convention: Threat or Challenge* (New York: Praeger, 1981), p. 75; see also, "Popular Action and the Budget," *U.S. News & World Report* (October 8, 1984), p. 106.

31. 17 U.S. 316, 319 (1819).

32. *Congressional Record*, 46 (1911) 2769.

33. Tribe, supra note 5, 638–639.

34. The argument that the original conventions of 1787 "ran away" has been repeated so often it has become something of a truism, and is used to imply that a second convention could do the same. The difficulty with this truism is that it is false, as proved in Chapter 2.

The truth is that even though the delegates went beyond the text of the Resolution of the Continental Congress, which authorized their deliberations, their actions were implicitly authorized. On February 21, 1787, Congress passed its resolution: "[W]hereas experience has evinced that there are defects in the present Confederation . . . and [a] Convention appearing to be the most probable means of establishing in these states a firm national government. . . . [O]n the second Monday in May next a Convention of delegates . . . be held at Philadelphia for the sole and express purpose of revising the Articles of Confederation and reporting to Congress and the several legislatures"

[*Documents Illustrative of the Formation of the Union of the American States,* H.R. Doc. No. 398, 69th Congress, 1st Sess. 45–6 (1927)].

35. Tribe, supra note 5, 638–639.

36. S.40, 99th Congress, 1st Sess. (1985). See Appendix I, infra, for a complete version of S.40.

37. A filibuster is not an unreasonable strategy for opponents. A motion to forward an amendment would require a simple majority vote. To stop a filibuster requires a three-fifths vote.

38. One piece of constitutional trivia may be of interest: if Puerto Rico were to become the fifty-first state, it would still take only thirty-four states to propose an amendment, but it would take thirty-nine to ratify one.

39. James Madison, *Federalist* No. 51 in *The Federalist Papers,* Clinton Rossiter, ed. (New York: Mentor Books, 1961), p. 325.

7

REFLECTIONS ON A BALANCED BUDGET AMENDMENT

As NOTED IN Chapter 4, the nearly successful drive to call a constitutional convention to consider a balanced budget amendment is the most recent and certainly most publicized effort to convene a national assembly to alter the Constitution. The campaign, which now appears to have fallen short of its goal by two states, has generated a plethora of scholarly studies and journalistic commentaries on the need for and the wisdom of the balanced budget amendment itself and a constitutional convention to consider and propose it. This chapter examines issues related to both the proposed amendment and convention and offers conclusions on this case study that are relevant to our more general thesis.

THE FEDERAL DEFICIT

The advocacy of an amendment to balance the federal government's budget increased in urgency as the United States' budget deficit multiplied at an alarming rate. For most of the nation's history, the federal government had operated "in the black." Except during wartime emergencies (1861–65, 1917–19) the United States managed to balance expenditures with receipts. Indeed, classical economic theory, which frowned on government debt, guided American public policy for the first century and half of the country's existence. But the Keynesian Revolution, with its economic justification for deficit financing, ushered in a new era for America's balance sheet. If Keynes supplied the theoretical rationale for deficit spending, the Great Depression presented a pragmatic need for it. Thus 1931—a year that saw the country plunge further into economic depression—signaled a watershed for the nation's budget policy.

Since 1931 the federal government has ended its fiscal year with a surplus only eleven times. It is an understatement to say that the deficit problem in the 1980s has grown more acute. Despite President Carter's promises and best efforts to balance the federal budget, the deficit stood at $59.6 billion when he turned the White House over to his successor.[1]

Ronald Reagan had campaigned on a theme of slashing the burgeoning deficit. His first inaugural address emphasized his commitment to returning the government's budget to its pre-1931 balance. He declared: "For decades we have piled deficit upon deficit, mortgaging our future and our children's future for the temporary convenience of the present. To continue this long trend is to guarantee tremendous social, cultural, political, and economic upheavals."[2] Nevertheless, by 1982 the deficit had grown to $110.6 billion; by 1983 to $195.4 billion. As Reagan's second term drew to a close, the federal deficit had mushroomed to an incomprehensible $3 *trillion*![3] Despite his rhetoric and good intentions, Reagan added more to the national debt than all previous presidencies combined. The now grossly unbalanced budget remained a hotly debated, if poorly understood, topic in 1988 presidential politics.

BALANCED BUDGET PROPOSALS

Hoping to avoid the more severe constitutional approach to the deficit, Congress has attempted statutory reform of the budget process, especially through its landmark legislation, the Budget and Impoundment Control Act of 1974. Congress also wrote into law as part of an International Monetary Fund loan program an amendment that required that total budget overlays of the federal government "shall not" exceed its receipts, beginning with fiscal year 1981.[4] (For the record, Congress approved a budget with a $50 billion deficit in 1981.)[5]

Continued pressure to address the growing deficit pushed Congress to pass the Balanced Budget and Emergency Deficit Control Act of 1985, commonly known as the Gramm-Rudman-Hollings Act, which was aimed at eliminating the federal deficit by 1991. The statute set maximum amounts for the federal deficit in each of fiscal years between 1986 and 1991.

More drastic, and supporters hope more effective, measures to reduce and eventually eliminate the deficit have been proffered in the form of constitutional amendments. Professor Aaron Wildavsky has outlined the two basic varieties of constitutional proposals. One requires a balanced budget; another limits the permissible tax revenue or the amount that can be spent, usually a proportion of the Gross National Product (GNP). (Examples of each approach are shown in Appendix III.) The most prominent proposal requires limiting spending to the prior year's amount times the proportionate increase or decrease in the GNP. Wildavsky's perceived distinction between the two has obvious political ramifications. He notes that a balanced budget "may be achieved through higher levels of taxation; it is compatible with larger government, providing the legislature is willing and able to raise revenue. The limitation amendment put[s] all the onus on spending; if the Gross National Product does not rise sufficiently to meet desired spending, it must be cut."[6]

Responding to public pressure, particularly the drive among the states to call a constitutional convention, the Senate Judiciary Subcommittee on the Constitution began in 1979 to study its own constitutional proposal to eliminate budget deficits. In 1981 the full Senate Committee on the Judiciary reported out a proposed amendment, Senate Joint Resolution 58 (S. J. Res. 58), which combined balanced budget prescriptions with taxing and spending limitations. One year later, and with White House support, the full Senate passed the measure by a vote of 69 to 31. S. J. Res. 58 proposed the following octet: (1) required Congress to approve a balanced budget before the beginning of each fiscal year; (2) allowed deficit spending only if two-thirds of the whole Congress voted to approve the shortfall; (3) required a three-fifths vote of the entire Congress to increase the debt limit; (4) proscribed an increase in the projection of total budget receipts in any fiscal year by more than the rate of increase of national income in the previous year; (5) defined total receipts as all receipts save those obtained by borrowing, and total expenditures as all those except for repayment of principal on debt; (6) provided congressional authority to implement and enforce the amendment "by appropriate legislation;" (7) established the principle that a declaration of war is a bona fide circumstance for waiving the amendment; and (8) ordered the amendment's implementation to begin the second fiscal year after ratification.[7] The House of Representatives' companion measure, H. J. Res. 350, failed to pass (236 to 187) in the fall of 1982.

Supporters of the balanced budget amendment have often admitted that pressure from the states was essential to force Congress to act on the measure. But as the early 1980s passed, the number of states that had passed resolutions calling for a constitutional convention to consider a balanced budget amendment appeared stalled at thirty-two, two states short of the required majority. Yet the issue was far from moot, and Congress continued to consider a number of budget balancing proposals. In May 1985 the Senate Judiciary Subcommittee on the Constitution approved, 5 to 0, a proposed amendment (S. J. Res. 13) that would have required a balanced budget within two years of state ratification. Supporters of the amendment had savored their victory for only a few hours when word came that the Connecticut Senate had voted to prevent consideration of a resolution to call for a constitutional convention on the balanced budget amendment. The National Taxpayers Union (NTU), a leading proponent of the amendment and a constitutional convention to consider it, was especially disappointed for Connecticut was considered a likely ally after its legislature shifted from Democratic to Republican control in the 1984 election. Moreover, its rejection of the amendment marked the seventh setback for balanced budget advocates attempting to urge two more states to pass convention call resolutions.[8]

In the summer of 1985 the Senate Judiciary Committee approved S. J. Res. 13 by a vote of 11 to 7. The proposed amendment was virtually identical to the 1982 version, S. J. Res. 58, which had passed in the Senate but failed in the House. The 1985 measure would have allowed deficit spending only during a declared war or upon a three-fifths vote of the whole Congress. A majority of the entire Congress would also have to approve any tax receipts increase that was more than the rate of increase of the "national income" the previous year. On the same day that the Judiciary Committee approved S. J. Res. 13, it also sent to the full Senate an alternative amendment (S. J. Res. 225) by a vote of 14 to 4. Like S. J. Res. 13, the second proposed measure required a balanced budget except during a declared war or if three-fifths of the Congress approved deficit spending. The alternative measure, however, contained language different from S. J. Res. 13, which some senators and the National Taxpayers Union argued would weaken its ability to prevent tax increases.[9]

In March 1986 the Senate rejected by a single vote a compromise version of the two amendments proposed by the Judiciary Committee. A change in Senate membership partially contributed to the crucial three-vote difference between the defeat of the 1986 amendment and the one successfully proposed in the Senate four years earlier. Moreover, passage of the Gramm-Rudman-Hollings Act in 1985 had arguably satisfied (at least temporarily) the Senate's urge to jump on the balanced budget bandwagon.[10]

Proponents of a convention to consider a balanced budget amendment received more distressing news in March 1986 when Kentucky's House of Representatives voted 70 to 28 for a resolution that called on Congress to balance the budget but did *not* call for a constitutional assembly on the subject. This defeat was the fifteenth loss by convention supporters since 1983, the year Missouri became the thirty-second state to call on Congress to convene a constitutional assembly.[11]

Nevertheless, the possibility of a state-initiated constitutional convention still loomed despite the inability of the movement to rise above the thirty-two-state plateau. The effort to reach the magic two-thirds majority required to convene a constitutional assembly experienced its most severe setback in April 1988 when the Alabama legislature rescinded its 1976 vote for a convention. The 1988 recision, which was passed over the veto of

Republican Governor Guy Hunt, was disputed by constitutional experts; but other states have putatively considered similar actions. At the very least, the movement to reverse resolutions calling for a convention put the balanced budget campaign on the defensive.

Still, as the deficits continued to skyrocket, the Senate made another effort to consider an amendment that would require the government to balance its budget. On May 25, 1988, the Senate Judiciary Subcommittee on the Constitution approved such a proposal, voting 3 to 2 to send the measure (S. J. Res. 11) to the full committee. Yet the subcommittee's chair and chief Democratic supporter of the amendment, Senator Paul Simon of Illinois, admitted that the odds were against passage of the proposal by the 99th Congress. At best, advocates of the balanced budget amendment hoped to reintroduce the measure in the new Congress, to convene in January 1989.[12]

The fits and starts of Congress' efforts to enact a balanced budget amendment reflect the vexatious cross-purposes under which individual members of Congress labor. In testimony before the Judiciary Committee's Subcommittee on the Constitution, Senator David Pryor (D-Ark.) graphically described the conflicting pressures applied by constituents. A group of them had traveled to Washington to meet with Pryor and present him with a list of projects they wanted for their district in Arkansas. As Pryor related the story to the subcommittee during its hearings on the balanced budget amendment, "The grand total of their requests came to a sum well over $6 million. As they were leaving the office, the parting comment was, 'Senator, there is one more item on our list. We want you to do all you can to balance the budget and cut down on Federal spending.' "[13] Undoubtedly, the 70 to 80 percent of Americans who have responded in recent public opinion polls that they favor a balanced budget amendment are sincere. Yet how many of the respondents would support the reduction or elimination of their pet government aid programs?

And while members of Congress feel the political squeeze between the proverbial rock and the hard place, the scholarly debate over the merits of the balanced budget amendment swirls about them. Yet because politics and economics are such inexact sciences (though their practitioners may hate to admit it!), the literature on the balanced budget issue often reflects the same ambivalence as Congress' activity on the subject. The proliferation of statements that are prefaced with "on the one hand," followed by the inevitable "on the other hand . . . " makes one appreciate President Harry Truman's exasperated plea for a "one-armed economist"! In addition to the economic pros and cons of the balanced budget debate, the issue eventually raises political and constitutional ramifications. Thus we examine the topic along its economic, political, and constitutional parameters.

ARGUMENTS SUPPORTING THE BALANCED BUDGET AMENDMENT

As we noted in Chapter 4, the first state petition to Congress calling for a constitutional convention to consider a balanced budget amendment was promulgated in 1957. But the big push on the issue came in the late 1970s, spurred on by rising deficits and double-digit inflation. In fact, James Davidson, chairman of the National Taxpayers Union, implied a direct link between the upward spirals of the federal deficit and the nation's inflation rate. In a 1979 *Christian Science Monitor* article, he wrote: "As the deficits have increased, so has the rate of inflation."[14] Economists have acknowledged this link between government deficits and inflation. Deficits create debts,[15] which may be financed by the government (barring tax increases) through borrowing or creating money. The latter approach, called "debt monetization," entails the conversion of government debt into money through the Federal Reserve System. The impact on inflation from such a policy is virtually the same as if the Treasury simply created money to cover the government's excess expenditures.[16]

According to economists who support a balanced budget amendment, the alternative to debt monetization, i.e., government borrowing, can also disrupt economic stability. An increase in government borrowing to finance the deficit results in a rise in interest rates, which, in turn, discourages private borrowing. The argument continues that because government borrowing tends to support consumption rather than investment, capital consumption will outpace capital accumulation. The reduction in our nation's capital, in effect, means that we are less prosperous than if borrowing had supported investment.[17] Economically, then, requiring a balanced budget makes good sense.

Not surprisingly, political arguments favoring a balanced budget reflect the economic components of the debate. Most proponents of the amendment, be they economists, political scientists, or practicing politicians, focus on the political bias favoring budget deficits in our democratic system. As noted above, the pre-Keynesian era had promoted a contrary bias in governmental budget policy, which avoided deficit spending in order to maintain a sound economy. Yet Keynes seemed to offer an economic rationale for promoting a healthy economy through government spending beyond the point of deficits, if need be. Thus politicians quite naturally seized the theoretical justification for their preferred budget policies of tax reductions and increased expenditures. As presidential candidate Walter Mondale discovered in 1984, American voters simply do not want to swallow the bitter pill of tax increases to reduce the deficit. Apparently, a majority of that electorate was happily reading George Bush's lips when he declared, "No new taxes" in the 1988 presidential campaign. Thus the combination of political pressures on individual members of Congress to reduce taxes while simultaneously increasing government expenditures has resulted in a federal budget policy that inevitably has produced record deficits.[18]

A number of politicians currently serving in the Senate have advocated a need to counteract the political bias toward spending through an amendment that would limit such spending in an effort to balance the budget. At the outset of the debate, Senator Orrin Hatch (R-Utah) insisted that

a balanced budget measure would reduce this bias toward spending by creating a countervailing political disadvantage for pro-spending votes that does not presently exist. For the first time, votes to increase spending would, under normal circumstances, have to be accompanied by votes to increase taxes or by votes to reduce other spending programs commensurately. Additional revenues that are presently available to elected officials, either through borrowing or through the automatic tax increases of inflation, and that make it easy for members of Congress to avoid politically difficult votes, would no longer be available.[19]

Hatch's political argument crosses the line into the constitutional realm at the point where the authority behind a balanced budget measure is considered. Before deficits became the norm in public financing, the balanced budget standard was a de facto component of our regime. As economists Richard Wagner and Robert Tollison argue, "[T]his political bias remained latent because our political process was constrained by the prevailing ethos, the belief that deficits were a sign of fiscal irresponsibility."[20] But when this ethos born of the classical school of economics gave way to economic depression, political interest groups, activist presidencies, and Keynesian theories, the new deficit ethos prevailed. Proponents of a balanced budget amendment maintain that only alteration of the Constitution itself will return the budgetary process to the status quo ante. They believe that the legislative process has fostered deficit spending and cannot be relied upon to establish a legislative solution to the problem.

Some supporters of the balanced budget amendment even argue that Congress cannot be trusted to propose the amendment. They perceive members of Congress as too short-sighted and self-interested to draft an effective proposal to present to the states. As Wagner and Tollison view the problem, allowing Congress to propose the balanced budget amendment is the legislative equivalent of letting the fox guard the chicken coop! The two economists have no fear of a "runaway" convention; indeed, they believe that a modern-day constitutional assembly would afford the nation a valuable intellectual and political exercise.[21]

Attorney Lawrence H. Silberman bases his argument in favor of a balanced budget amendment and a convention to propose it on slightly more theoretical grounds. At a 1979 American Enterprise Institute conference on the Constitution and the budget, he posited: "If one takes the view that political freedom does depend on economic freedom, then one must conclude that it is perfectly appropriate under our Constitution to call a convention, in part, to consider the degree of economic liberty, which is another way of phrasing the degree to which the government can appropriate money from its citizens for, among other purposes, the redistribution of income."[22]

To summarize, in economic terms the balanced budget amendment is viewed by its supporters as necessary for lowering inflation, decreasing interest rates, and promoting accumulation of capital. In short, stabilizing the economy is the goal of the amendment's proponents. Moreover, they believe that political bias in our system toward spending must be offset by a countervailing mandate to keep spending under control. Finally, the amendment's supporters argue that only a *constitutional* mandate will be strong enough to bring America's balance sheet "into the black."

ARGUMENTS OPPOSING THE BALANCED BUDGET AMENDMENT

Arguments against a balanced budget amendment predict dismal economic results if such a proposal is adopted. Economist Robert Eisner has warned that "a budget balanced by current Federal rules of accounting is an invitation to economic disaster. If achieved solely by expenditure cuts, it would be likely to devastate public investment. And, however accomplished, by reducing aggregate demand and purchasing power, it would threaten the worst recession or depression in half a century."[23] Alice Rivlin, while director of the Congressional Budget Office, expressed similar concerns in 1979 as the country struggled through a recessionary period. She maintained that attempts to balance the budget during such a downturn in the business cycle "will almost certainly make the recession significantly worse." She continued: "Deficits occur automatically in recession since declining incomes produce lower Federal revenues and spending for unemployment compensation rises. At such a moment, raising taxes or cutting spending in order to balance the budget would reduce aggregate demand further and throw additional people out of work."[24]

Eisner's and Rivlin's arguments have been generally stated as a problem of the proposed amendment's inflexibility. Opponents of the amendment argue that the federal budget should not be placed in a constitutional straitjacket that would not allow it to react to economic vagaries.[25] Moreover, as Herbert Stein, former chairman of President Nixon's Council of Economic Advisers, has written, "There is no objective way to determine how much the nation should forgo current government services and private consumption in order to make the future national income greater . . . The desirable size of the surplus or deficit is not fixed forever. That is why it should not be incorporated in a constitutional amendment. The choice of a surplus or deficit target is a political decision to be made from time to time in the light of long-run growth considerations."[26]

The enforceability issue, another argument against the amendment, questions who would implement the balanced budget prescriptions even if there was a consensus on their economic wisdom and viability. Political, legal, and constitutional controversies abound. Would there be a penalty for not balancing the budget? If so, who would pay? Should the courts determine whether standards in a balanced budget amendment had been met or would the judiciary eschew the issue by invoking the political question doctrine?[27] Federal Appeals Court Judge Ralph K. Winter, before going on the bench, raised the possibility that the amendment would be unenforceable because no one could sue Congress if it failed to follow the amendment. He pointed out that the criteria for establishing standing to bring suit are in the Constitution; therefore, a balanced budget amendment must create the standing because Congress cannot do so by mere legislation.[28]

Opponents of the balanced budget amendment also have addressed its supporters' primary political argument that the budgetary process itself is biased toward spending and deficit financing. They counter that the budgetary process per se is neutral but that the upward spiral of government spending and deficits results from the will of the people as translated by their elected representatives in Washington. The opposition claims that an amendment is unnecessary because "there are no con-

stitutional barriers or obstacles to Congress' control of federal
spending. The Constitution already gives Congress plenary
power in this area. Congress can balance the budget if a majority of Congress votes to do so."[29] In the same vein, Nobel Prize
winner Paul Samuelson, one of 500 economists who signed an
open letter opposing a balanced budget amendment, reasoned
that "there is no inherent flaw in our checks and balances and
division of responsibility among the legislative, executive, and
judicial branches of government that makes inevitable a process
of 'logrolling' designed to swell the level of expenditures and
taxes beyond that truly desired by the effective majority of the
electorate."[30]

Thus the problems of government spending and deficits do
not result from an institutional defect that can be corrected by
altering the Constitution. Rather, in our republican system, the
people must be willing to accept less from the government and
convey that message to their representatives. But the undertak-
ing is a painful one. One of the most poignant descriptions of
the Hobson's choice faced by a member of Congress when he
attempts to slash spending was offered by Representative David
R. Obey (D-Wis.) several years ago. In concluding that he must
oppose an amendment to balance the budget, he asked, "What
happens to services that Government provides to business, to
workers, to travelers, to consumers, to local governments, you
name it, ad nauseam, if the budget for these services must move
in unison with economic changes?"[31] Obey actually simulated a
belt-tightening budget with a program-by-program cut in government outlays. In so doing, he managed to pare $38 billion
from the federal budget. Yet the Congressional Budget Office
reported that his across-the-board cuts in spending would result in a $60 billion drop in GNP, a 1 percent rise in unem-
ployment, and a reduction in inflation of only 0.1 percent.[32]

Yet even if it could be proved that budget deficits resulted
from a systemic defect in our political regime, a number of
arguments militate against incorporating a balanced budget requirement into our Constitution. The first relates to economic
reasoning regarding a constitutional amendment's inflexibility.
Of course, supporters of the amendment find its beauty in its

very inflexibility. They do not want the government's balance sheet left to the mercy of the political process.

Others believe that the need for a budgetary process that responds to economic exigencies argues against amending the Constitution along these lines. If the amendment were drafted in more flexible language, it would likely run afoul of the "vice of vagueness." Lack of specificity would also invite more judicial interpretation and increase the likelihood of ineffectiveness. The possibility of "unseemly disputes over the meaning of the amendment will discredit the very Constitution it is supposed to strengthen."[33]

On a more general, but related, point, opponents of the amendment focus on the problems associated with "constitutionalizing" economic policy. They argue that our governing document was intended to embody fundamental law, not the economic orthodoxy of the day. Some opponents have even compared a potential balanced budget amendment with the ill-fated Eighteenth Amendment as an example of the Constitution's inability to engineer social or economic goals.[34] And, of course, the debate prompts echoes of Justice Oliver Wendell Holmes's oft-quoted admonition in *Lochner v. New York*[35] that the Constitution (in that case the Fourteenth Amendment) does not embody voguish economic theories.

CONCLUDING THOUGHTS ON A BALANCED BUDGET AMENDMENT AND A CONSTITUTIONAL CONVENTION

The fact that our economic landscape has changed so dramatically in the ten short years since the start of the balanced budget campaign may constitute the most damning evidence against writing a balanced budget requirement into our enduring fundamental law. Most proponents of the amendment in the late 1970s used double-digit inflation as a starting point for their advocacy of balanced budgets. Senator Richard C. Lugar (R-Ind.), a staunch supporter of the amendment, speculated in 1979 that if inflation became less of a problem for the American people, "the balanced budget amendment idea will eventually dissipate and fail."[36] Lugar's speculation foretold the stalling of the balanced budget amendment movement that has coincided with the lowering of the inflation rate to below 5 percent in the late 1980s. Unfortunately, despite the positive direction of the nation's leading economic indicators as the 1980s waned, the federal deficit has continued to escalate. Yet it now comprises only about 3 percent of the GNP, whereas just a few years ago it was 6 percent of the GNP.[37]

Thus the dire predictions for the economy propounded by the amendment's supporters have failed to materialize. Whereas many of the economic justifications for the amendment have weakened, the political and constitutional arguments against it remain strong. Those who have concluded that an amendment to the U.S. Constitution is not the answer to solving the conundrum of the federal deficit, obviously see no need to convoke a constitutional convention on *this* particular subject. Unlike many opponents of the balanced budget amendment, however, the authors do not fear the constitutional convention process per se.[38] Indeed, we want it to remain a viable part of our constitutional framework should we ever need it to address a national problem more amenable to constitutional alterations. Campaign finance reform strikes us as an illustrative issue. At the very least, we believe that the threat of a constitutional convention must remain realistic if for no other reason than to spur Congress to act when it otherwise would fail to do so.

NOTES

1. See Richard H. Fink and Jack C. High, eds., *A Nation in Debt: Economists Debate the Federal Budget Deficit* (Frederick, MD: University Publications of America, Inc., 1987), pp. xiii–xxvii, for an excellent introduction to and history of the deficit issue.

2. As quoted in Robert Eisner, *How Real Is the Federal Deficit?* (New York: The Free Press, 1986), p. v.

3. Fink and High, *A Nation in Debt*, p. xiii.

4. P. L. 95–435. Cited by Alvin Rabuska, "A Compelling Case for a Constitutional Amendment to Balance the Budget and Limit Taxes," in Fink and High, *A Nation in Debt*, pp. 213–214.

5. Ibid.

6. Aaron Wildavsky, *The Politics of the Budgetary Process*, 4th ed. (Boston: Little, Brown, 1984), pp. 257–258.

7. This summary of S. J. Res. 58 was provided by Raymond J. Saulnier in "Do We Need a Balanced Budget Amendment to the Constitution?" *Presidential Studies Quarterly*, 28 (Winter 1988), 158.

8. "Balanced Budget Amendment Advances Here, Loses There," *Congressional Quarterly Weekly Report* (May 18, 1985), pp. 933–934.

9. "Two Balanced-Budget Plans Approved by Senate Judiciary," *Congressional Quarterly Weekly Report*, 43, No. 20 (July 13, 1985), 1393.

10. Six senators switched their votes on the issue between 1982 and 1986. Four who had voted aye initially changed to nay on the second amendment: Quentin Burdick (D-N.D.); Robert C. Byrd (D-W.Va.); Mark O. Hatfield (R-Ore.); and Robert T. Stafford (R-Vt.) Two others changed their votes from nay in 1982 to aye in 1986: Wendell H. Ford (D-Ky.) and Claiborne Pell (D-R.I.). Stafford and Burdick specifically attributed their switch to a desire to allow Gramm-Rudman-Hollings a chance to lower the deficit before resorting to a constitutional amendment. Another change in the vote total came from Frank F. Lautenberg (D-N.J.), who had replaced Nicholas Brady (R-N.J.) and who voted oppositely to his predecessor. "Balanced Budget Amendment," *1986 Congressional Quarterly Almanac*, p. 578; Saulnier, "Do We Need a Balanced Budget Amendment?" p. 158.

11. "Senate to Vote March 25 on Balanced Budget," *Congressional Quarterly Weekly Report*, 44 No. 10 (March 15, 1986), 590.

12. "Economic Notes: Balanced Budget," *Congressional Quarterly Weekly Report*, 46, No. 22 (May 28, 1988), 1443.

13. As quoted in Wildavsky, *The Politics of the Budgetary Process*, p. 262.

14. Cited in U.S. Congress, Senate Committee on the Judiciary, *Constitutional Convention Procedures, Hearing before the Subcommittee on the Constitution on S. 3, S. 520, and S. 1710.* 96th Cong., 1st sess. (1979) p. 469.

15. For a simple and practical distinction between deficits and debts, see Eisner, *How Real Is the Federal Deficit?* pp. 219–220.

16. Richard E. Wagner and Robert D. Tollison, "Balanced Budgets, Fiscal Responsibility, and the Constitution," in Fink and High, *A Nation in Debt*, p. 189.

17. Ibid., pp. 185–187.

18. Ibid., p. 185.

19. Opening statement of Senator Orrin G. Hatch of Utah, *Hearings on a Proposed Balanced Budget Constitutional Amendment*, Subcommittee on the Constitution, Senate Judiciary Committee, March 11, 1981. As quoted in Wildavsky, *The Politics of the Budgetary Process*, pp. 260–261.

20. Wagner and Tollison, "Balanced Budgets, Fiscal Responsibility, and the Constitution," p. 185.

21. Ibid., p. 205. The National Taxpayers Union has followed the same line of reasoning. See James Davidson's statement as quoted in *Constitutional Convention Procedures*, p. 470.

22. Lawrence H. Silberman, "The Case for a General Constitutional Convention," in W.S. Moore and Rudolph G. Penner, eds., *The Constitution and the Budget* (Washington, DC: American Enterprise Institute for Public Policy Research, 1980), p. 15.

23. Eisner, *How Real Is the Federal Deficit?* p. 179.

24. Alice Rivlin, hearings before the Subcommittee on the Constitution of the Committee on the Judiciary, U.S. Senate, on Proposed Constitutional Amendment to Balance the Federal Budget, March 12, May 23, July 25, October 5 and 11, and November 1, 1979 (Serial No. 96–41), p. 261. As quoted in Wildavsky, *The Politics of the Budgetary Process*, p. 266.

25. Saulnier, "Do We Need a Balanced Budget Amendment?" p. 159.

26. Herbert Stein, "The Significance of Budget Deficits," in High and Fink, *A Nation in Debt*, pp. 240–241.

27. Wildavsky raises several of these issues related to enforcement in his *The Politics of the Budgetary Process*, pp. 272–274. See also Rudolph G. Penner, "Constitutional and Statutory Approaches," in Albert T. Sommers, ed., *Reconstructing the Federal Budget: A Trillion Dollar Quandary* (New York: Praeger, 1984), pp. 234–235.

28. Ralph K. Winter, "The Feasibility of an Amendment: Some Legal and Political Considerations," in Moore and Penner, eds., *The Constitution and the Budget*, pp. 142–143.

29. Marshall Beil, spokesman for the Committee on Federal Legislation of the New York City Bar, Hearings Before the Subcommittee on the Constitution, p. 26. As quoted in Wildavsky, *The Politics of the Budgetary Process*, p. 264.

30. Samuelson, Hearings Before the Subcommittee on the Constitution, p. 559. As quoted in Wildavsky, *The Politics of the Budgetary Process*, p. 265.

31. David R. Obey, "The Balanced Budget: A View from Congress," in Moore and Penner, *The Constitution and the Budget*, p. 130.

32. Ibid., p. 133.

33. Wildavsky, *The Politics of the Budgetary Process*, p. 271. Although Wildavsky reports this potential flaw in the amendment, he ultimately expresses his support for constitutional spending limits, p. 279.

34. See Meredith McCoy's and Senator John Culver's respective statements in *Constitutional Convention Procedures*, pp. 357–360, 470–

471, and Mancur Olson, "Is the Balanced Budget Amendment Another Form of Prohibition?" and Obey, "The Balanced Budget" in Moore and Penner, *The Constitution and the Budget*, pp. 91–94, 130.

35. 198 U.S. 45 (1905).

36. Richard G. Lugar, "Problems and Prospects of Budget Balance," in Moore and Penner, *The Constitution and the Budget*, p. 125.

37. Figures determined by economist Robert Eisner of Northwestern University and reported by Tom Wicker, "His Lips Speak Truth," Louisville *Courier-Journal*, December 21, 1988, p. A15.

38. See, e.g., Gerald Gunther, "The Convention Method of Amending the United States Constitution," *Georgia Law Review*, 14 (Fall), 1979.

Appendix I

PROPOSED LEGISLATION TO ESTABLISH CONVENTION PROCEDURES

99th CONGRESS
1st SESSION
S.40

To provide procedures for calling federal constitutional conventions under article V for the purpose of proposing amendments to the United States Constitution.

IN THE SENATE OF THE UNITED STATES
January 3, 1985
MR. HATCH (for himself, MR. THURMOND, and MR. DECONCINI) introduced the following bill, which was read twice and referred to the Committee on the Judiciary.

Be it enacted by the Senate and House of Representatives of the United States of America in Congress Assembled, That this Act may be cited as the "Constitutional Convention Implementation Act of 1985."

APPLICATIONS FOR CONSTITUTIONAL CONVENTION

SEC. 2. (a) The legislature of a State, in making application to the Congress for a constitutional convention under article V of the Constitution of the United States, for the purpose of proposing one or more specific amendments, shall adopt a resolution pursuant to this Act stating, in substance, that the legislature requests the calling of a convention for the purpose of proposing one or more specific amendments to the Constitution of the United States and stating the subject matter of the amendment or amendments to be proposed.

(b) The procedures provided by this Act are required to be used whenever application is made to the Congress, under article V of the Constitution of the United States, for the calling of any convention for the purposes of proposing one or more specific amendments to the Constitution of the United States, each applying State stating in the terms of its application the subject matter of the amendment or amendments to be proposed. This Act is not intended to apply to applications requesting a convention for any other purpose under article V of the Constitution.

APPLICATION PROCEDURE

SEC. 3. (a) The rules of procedure governing the adoption or withdrawal of a resolution pursuant to section 2 and section 5 of this Act are determinable by the State legislature, except that the assent of the Governor as to any application or withdrawal shall be unnecessary.

(b) Questions concerning compliance with the rules governing the adoption or withdrawal of a State resolution cognizable under this Act are determinable by the State legislature, except that questions concerning the fact of final approval of such resolution by no less than a majority vote of each House of such legislature shall be determinable by the Congress of the United States.

TRANSMITTAL OF APPLICATIONS

SEC. 4. (a) Within thirty days after the effective date of the resolution adopted by the legislature of a State calling for a constitutional convention, the secretary of state of the State, or, if there be no such officer, the person who is charged by the State law with such function, shall transmit to the Congress of the United States two copies of the application, one addressed to the President of the Senate and one to the Speaker of the House of Representatives.

(b) Each Copy of the application so made by any State shall contain—

(1) the title of the resolution, the exact text of the resolution signed by the presiding officer of each house of the State legislature, the date on which the legislature adopted the resolution, and a certificate of the secretary of state of

the State, or such other person as is charged by the State law with such function, certifying that the application accurately sets forth the text of the resolution; and

(2) to the extent practicable, and if desired, a list of all State applications in effect on the date of adoption whose subject matter are substantially the same as the subject matter set forth in the application.

(c) Within ten days after receipt of a copy of any such application, the President of the Senate and Speaker of the House of Representatives shall report to the House of which he is presiding officer, identifying the State making application, the subject matter of the application, and the number of States then having made application on such subject. The President of the Senate and Speaker of the House of Representatives shall jointly cause copies of such application to be sent to the presiding officer of each house of the legislature of every other State and to each Member of the Senate and House of Representatives of the Congress of the United States.

EFFECTIVE PERIOD OF APPLICATION

SEC. 5. (a) An application submitted to the Congress by a State, unless sooner withdrawn by the State legislature, shall remain effective for the lesser of the period specified in such application by the State legislature or for a period of seven calendar years after the date it is received by the Congress, except that whenever within a period of seven calendar years two-thirds or more of the several States have each submitted an application calling for a constitutional convention on the same subject matter all such applications shall remain in effect until the Congress has taken action on a concurrent resolution, pursuant to section 6 of this Act, calling for a constitutional convention: *Provided however*, that those applications which have not been before the Congress for more than twelve years on the effective date of this Act shall be effective for a period of not less than two years.

(b) A State may withdraw its application calling for a constitutional convention by adopting and transmitting to the Congress a resolution of withdrawal in conformity with the procedures specified in sections 3 and 4 of this Act, except that no such withdrawal shall be effective as to any valid application made for a constitutional convention upon any subject after the date on which two-thirds or more of the State legislatures have valid applications pending before the Congress seeking amendments on the same subject matter.

CALLING OF A CONSTITUTIONAL CONVENTION

SEC. 6. (a) It shall be the duty of the Secretary of the Senate and the Clerk of the House of Representatives to maintain a record of all applications received by the President of the Senate and Speaker of the House of Representatives from States for the calling of a constitutional convention upon each subject matter. Whenever applications made by two-thirds or more of the States with respect to the same subject matter have been received, the Secretary and the Clerk shall so report within five days, in writing to the officer to whom those applications were transmitted, and such officer, no later than the fifth day subsequent to the receipt of such report during which the House of which he is an officer is in session, shall announce its substance on the floor of such House. It shall then be the duty of such House to determine whether there are in effect valid applications made by two-thirds of the States with respect to the same subject matter. If either House of the Congress determines, upon a consideration of any such report or of a concurrent resolution agreed to by the other House of the Congress, that there are in effect valid applications made by two-thirds or more of the States for the calling of a constitutional convention upon the same subject matter, it shall be the duty of that House, within forty-five calendar days following the day on which the report of the Clerk or the Secretary was announced on the floor of that House, to agree to a concurrent resolution calling for the convening of a Federal constitutional convention upon that subject matter. Each such concurrent resolution shall (1) designate the place and time of meeting of the convention, and (2) set forth the subject matter of the amendment or amendments for the consideration of which the convention is called. A copy of each such concurrent resolution agreed to by both Houses of the Congress shall be transmitted forthwith to the Governor and to the presiding officer of each house of the legislature of each State.

(b) The convention shall be convened not later than eight months after adoption of the resolution.

DELEGATES

SEC. 7. (a) In each State two delegates shall be elected on an at-large basis and one delegate shall be elected from each congressional district in the manner provided by State law. No Senator or Representative, or person holding an office or trust or profit under the United

States, shall be elected as delegate. Any vacancy occurring in a State delegation shall be filled by appointment of the legislature of that State.

(b) The secretary of state of each State, or, if there be no such officer, the person charged by State law to perform such function, shall certify to the President of the Senate and the Speaker of the House of Representatives the name of each delegate elected or appointed by the legislature of the State pursuant to this section.

(c) Delegates shall in all cases, except treason, felony, and breach of the peace, be privileged from arrest during their attendance at a session of the convention, and in going to and returning from the same; and for any speech or debate in the convention they shall not be questioned in any other place.

CONVENING THE CONVENTION

SEC. 8. (a) The President pro tempore of the United States Senate and the Speaker of the United States House of Representatives shall jointly convene the constitutional convention. They shall administer the oath of office of the delegates to the convention and shall preside until the delegates elect a presiding officer who shall preside thereafter. Before taking his seat each delegate shall subscribe to an oath by which he shall be committed during the conduct of the convention to comply with the Constitution of the United States. Further proceedings of the convention shall be conducted in accordance with such rules, not inconsistent with this Act, as the convention may adopt by vote of three-fifths of the number of delegates who have subscribed to the oath of office.

(b) There is hereby authorized to be appropriated such sums as may be necessary for the payment of the expenses of the convention, including payment to each delegate of an amount of pay equal to that for Members of Congress prorated for the term of the convention, as well as necessary travel expenses for such delegates. In the event that such sums are not appropriated in a timely manner, or are appropriated subject to additional conditions, the convention shall be authorized to apportion its costs among the States.

(c) The Administrator of General Services shall provide such facilities, and the Congress and each executive department, agency, or authority of the United States shall provide such information and assistance as the convention may require, upon written request made by the elected presiding officer of the convention.

PROCEDURES OF THE CONVENTION

SEC. 9. (a) In voting on any question before the convention, including the proposal of amendments, each delegate shall have one vote.

(b) The convention shall keep a daily verbatim record of its proceedings and publish the same. The vote of the delegates on any question shall be entered on the record.

(c) The convention shall terminate its proceedings within six months after convening unless the period is extended by concurrent resolution of the Congress of the United States upon request from the convention.

(d) Within thirty days after the termination of the proceedings of the convention, the presiding officer shall transmit to the Archivist of the United States all records of official proceedings of the convention.

PROPOSAL OF AMENDMENTS

SEC. 10. No convention called under this Act may propose any amendment or amendments of a subject matter different from that stated in the concurrent resolution calling the convention.

APPROVAL BY THE CONGRESS AND TRANSMITTAL TO THE STATES FOR RATIFICATION

SEC. 11. (a) The presiding officer of the convention shall, within thirty days after the termination of its proceedings, submit to the Congress the exact text of any amendment or amendments agreed upon by the convention.

(b) Whenever a constitutional convention called under this Act has transmitted to the Congress a proposed amendment to the Constitution, the Congress shall in as expeditious a manner as possible, but in any case within six months thereafter, adopt a concurrent resolution—

(i) directing the Administrator of General Services to transmit forthwith to each of the several States a duly certified copy thereof, and a copy of any concurrent resolution agreed to by both Houses of Congress which prescribes the mode in which such amendment shall be ratified and the time within which such amendment shall be ratified in the event that the amendment itself contains no such provision. In no case shall such a resolution prescribe a period for ratification of less than four years; or

(ii) stating that the Congress does not direct the submission of such proposed amendment to the States because such proposed amendment relates to or includes subject matter which differs from or was not included in the subject matter named or described in the concurrent resolution of the Congress by which the convention was called.

(c) In the event that the Congress has not passed a concurrent resolution under subsection (b)(i) within the time prescribed therein, during the thirty days following any State may commence an action under section 15 of this Act seeking a declaration that the proposed amendment is consistent with the concurrent resolution by the Congress by which the convention was called and directing its submission to the States for ratification.

(d) Notwithstanding the issuance of such order, the mandate of the court shall not issue prior to the expiration of the first period of thirty days following the date on which such order is issued. Congress may during such thirty-day period, adopt a concurrent resolution prescribing the mode in which such amendment shall be ratified, and the time within which the amendment shall be ratified in the event that the amendment itself contains no such provision. In no case shall such a resolution prescribe a period for ratification of less than four years.

(e) In the event that the Congress has not adopted a concurrent resolution under subsection (d) within the time prescribed therein, the mandate for such order shall issue forthwith. The mode for ratification in such case shall be by action of the legislatures of three-fourths of the States within a period of seven years, unless the amendment itself contains a different period.

RATIFICATION OF PROPOSED AMENDMENTS

SEC. 12. (a) Any amendment proposed by the convention and submitted to the States in accordance with the provisions of this Act shall be valid for all intents and purposes as part of the Constitution of the United States when duly ratified by three-fourths of the States in the manner and within the time specified consistent with the provisions of article V of the Constitution of the United States.

(b) The secretary of state of the State, or if there be no such officer, the person who is charged by State law with such function, shall transmit a certified copy of the State action ratifying any proposed amendment to the Administrator of General Services.

RESCISSION OF RATIFICATIONS

SEC. 13. (a) Any State may rescind its ratification of a proposed amendment by the same procedures by which it ratified the proposed amendment, unless other procedures are specified by such State, except that no State may rescind when there are existing valid ratifications of such amendment by three-fourths of the States.

(b) Any State may ratify a proposed amendment even though it previously may have rejected the same proposal or may have rescinded a prior ratification thereof.

PROCLAMATION OF CONSTITUTIONAL AMENDMENTS

SEC. 14. The Administrator of General Services, when three-fourths of the several States have ratified a proposed amendment to the Constitution of the United States, shall issue a proclamation that the amendment is a part of the Constitution of the United States.

JUDICIAL REVIEW

SEC. 15. (a) Any State aggrieved by any determination or finding, or by any failure of Congress to make a determination or finding within the periods provided, under section 6 or section 11 of this Act may bring an action in the Supreme Court of the United States against the Secretary of the Senate and the Clerk of the House of Representatives or, where appropriate, the Administrator of General Services, and such other parties as may be necessary to afford the relief sought. Such an action shall be given priority on the Court's docket.

(b) Every claim arising under this Act shall be barred unless suit is filed thereon within sixty days after such claim first arises.

(c) The right to review by the Supreme Court provided under subsection (a) does not limit or restrict the right to judicial review of any other determination or decision made under this Act or such review as is otherwise provided by the Constitution or any other law in the United States.

EFFECTIVE DATE OF AMENDMENTS

Sec. 16. An amendment proposed to the Constitution of the United States shall be effective from the date specified therein or, if no date is specified, then on the date on which the last State necessary to constitute three-fourths of the States of the United States, as provided for in article V, has ratified the same.

Appendix II

THE FEDERALIST NO. 40[1]
JAMES MADISON, JANUARY 18, 1788

To the People of the State of New York.

The *second* point to be examined is, whether the Convention were authorised to frame and propose this mixed Constitution.

The powers of the Convention ought in strictness to be determined, by an inspection of the commissions given to the members by their respective constituents. As all of these however had reference, either to the recommendation from the meeting at Annapolis in September, 1786, or to that from Congress in February, 1787, it will be sufficient to recur to these particular acts.

The act from Annapolis recommends the "appointment of commissioners to take into consideration, the situation of the United States, to devise *such further provisions* as shall appear to them necessary to render the Constitution of the Federal Government *adequate to the exigencies of the Union*; and to report such an act for that purpose, to the United States in Congress assembled, as when agreed to by them, and afterwards confirmed by the Legislature of every State, will effectually provide for the same."

The recommendatory act of Congress is in the words following:

---

[1]From *The New-York Packet*, January 18, 1788. This essay appeared on January 19 in both *The Independent Journal* and *The Daily Advertiser*. It was numbered 40 in the McLean edition and 39 in the newspapers.

"Whereas there is provision in the articles of confederation and perpetual Union, for making alterations therein, by the assent of a Congress of the United States, and of the Legislatures of the several States: And whereas experience hath evinced, that there are defects in the present confederation, as a means to remedy which, several of the States, and *particularly the State of New York*, by express instructions to their delegates in Congress, have suggested a Convention for the purposes expressed in the following resolution; and such Convention appearing to be the most probable mean of establishing in these States, *a firm national government*.

"Resolved, That in the opinion of Congress, it is expedient, that on the 2d Monday in May next, a Convention of delegates, who shall have been appointed by the several States, be held at Philadelphia for the sole and express purpose of *revising the articles of confederation*, and reporting to Congress and the several Legislatures, such *alterations and provisions therein*, as shall, when agreed to in Congress, and confirmed by the States, render the Federal Constitution *adequate to the exigencies of government* and *the preservation of the Union*."

From these two acts it appears, 1st. that the object of the Convention was to establish in these States, *a firm national government*; 2d. that this Government was to be such as would be *adequate to the exigencies of government and the preservation of the Union*; 3d. that these purposes were to be effected by *alterations and provisions in the articles of confederation*, as it is expressed in the act of Congress, or by *such further provisions as should appear necessary*, as it stands in the recommendatory act from Annapolis; 4th. that the alterations and provisions were to be reported to Congress, and to the States, in order to be agreed to be the former, and confirmed by the latter.

From a comparison and fair construction of these several modes of expression, is to be deduced the authority, under which the Convention acted. They were to frame a *national government*, adequate to the *exigencies of government* and *of the Union*, and to reduce the articles of confederation into such form as to accomplish these purposes.

There are two rules of construction dictated by plain reason, as well as founded on legal axioms. The one is, that every part of the expression ought, if possible, to be allowed some meaning, and be made to conspire to some common end. The other is, that where the several parts cannot be made to coincide, the less important should give way to the more important part; the means should be sacrificed to the end, rather than the end to the means.

Suppose then that the expressions defining the authority of the Convention, were irreconcilably at variance with each other; that a *national* and *adequate government* could not possibly, in the judgment of the Convention, be effected by *alterations* and *provisions* in the *articles of confederation*, which part of the definition ought to have been embraced, and which rejected? Which was the more important, which the less important part? Which the end, which the means? Let the most scrupulous expositors of delegated powers: Let the most inveterate objectors against those exercised by the Convention, answer these questions. Let them declare, whether it was of most importance to the happiness of the people of America, that the articles of confederation should be disregarded, and an adequate government be provided, and the Union preserved; or that an adequate government should be omitted, and the articles of confederation preserved. Let them declare, whether the preservation of these articles was the end for securing which a reform of the government was to be introduced as the means; or whether the establishment of a government, adequate to the national happiness, was the end at which these articles themselves originally aimed, and to which they ought, as insufficient means, to have been sacrificed.

But is it necessary to suppose that these expressions are absolutely irreconcilable to each other; that no *alterations* or *provisions* in *the articles of the confederation*, could possibly mould them into a national and adequate government; into such a government as has been proposed by the Convention?

No stress it is presumed will in this case be laid on the *title*, a change of that could never be deemed an exercise of ungranted power. *Alterations* in the body of the instrument, are expressly authorised. *New provisions* therein are also expressly authorised. Here then is a power to change the title; to insert new articles; to alter old ones. Must it of necessity be admitted that this power is infringed, so long as a part of the old articles remains? Those who maintain the affirmative, ought at least to mark the boundary between authorised and usurped innovations, between that degree of change, which lies within the compass of *alterations and further provisions*; and that which amounts to a *transmutation* of the government. Will it be said that the alterations ought not to have touched the substance of the confederation? The States would never have appointed a Convention with so much solemnity, nor described its objects with so much latitude, if some *substantial* reform had not been in contemplation. Will it be said that the *fundamental principles* of the confederation were not within the purview of the Convention, and ought not to have been varied? I ask what are these principles? Do they require that in the establishment of the Constitution, the States should be regarded as distinct and independent sovereigns? They are so regarded by the Constitution proposed. Do they require that the members of the government should derive their appointment from the Legislatures, not from the people of the State? One branch of the new government is to be appointed by these Legislatures; and under the confederation the delegates to Congress *may all* be appointed immediately by the people, and in two states[2] are actually so appointed. Do they require that the powers of the Government should act on the States, and not immediately on individuals? In some instances, as has been shown, the powers of the new Government will act on the States in their collective characters. In some instances also those of the existing Government act immediately on individuals. In cases of capture, of piracy, of the post-office, of coins, weights and measures, of trade with the Indians, of claims under grants of land by different States, and above all, in the case of trials by Courts-martial in the army and navy, by which death may be inflicted without the intervention of a jury, or even a civil Magistrate; in all these cases the powers of the confederation operate immediately on the persons and interests of individual citizens. Do these fundamental principles require particularly, that no tax should be levied without the intermediate agency of the States! The confederation itself authorises a direct tax to a certain extent on the post-office. The power of coinage has been so construed by Congress, as to levy a tribute immediately from that source also. But pretermitting these instances, was it not an acknowledged object of the Convention, and the universal expectation of the people, that the regulation of trade should be submitted to the general government in such a form as would render it an immediate source of general revenue? Had not Congress repeatedly recommended this measure as not inconsistent with the fundamental principles of the confederation? Had not every State but one, had not New-York herself, so far complied with the plan of Congress, as to recognize the *principle* of the innovation? Do these principles in fine require that the powers of the general government should be limited, and that beyond this limit, the States should be left in possession of their sovereignty and independence? We have seen that in the new government as in the old, the general powers are limited, and that the States in all unenumerated cases, are left in the enjoyment of their sovereign and independent jurisdiction.

The truth is, that the great principles of the Constitution proposed by the Convention, may be considered less as absolutely new, than as the expansion of principles which are found in the articles of Confederation. The misfortune under the latter system has been that these

[2]Connecticut and Rhode Island. (Publius)

principles are so feeble and confined as to justify all the charges of inefficiency which have been urged against it; and to require a degree of enlargement which gives to the new system, the aspect of an entire transformation of the old.

In one particular it is admitted that the Convention have departed from the tenor of their commission. Instead of reporting a plan requiring the confirmation *of the Legislatures of all the States*, they have reported a plan which is to be confirmed by the *people*, and may be carried into effect by *nine States only*. It is worthy of remark, that this objection, though the most plausible, has been the least urged in the publications which have swarmed against the Convention. The forbearance can only have proceeded from an irresistible conviction of the absurdity of subjecting the fate of 12 States, to the perverseness of corruption of a thirteenth; from the example of inflexible opposition given by a *majority* of 1–60th of the people of America,[3] to a measure approved and called for by the voice of twelve States comprising 59–60ths of the people; an example still fresh in the memory and indignation of every citizen who has felt for the wounded honor and prosperity of his country. As this objection, therefore, has been in a manner waived by those who have criticised the powers of the Convention, I dismiss it without further observation.

The *third* point to be enquired into is, how far considerations of duty arising out of the case itself, could have supplied any defect of regular authority.

In the preceding enquiries, the powers of the Convention have been analised and tried with the same rigour, and by the same rules, as if they had been real and final powers, for the establishment of a Constitution for the United States. We have seen, in what manner they have borne the trial, even on that supposition. It is time now to recollect, that the powers were merely advisory and recommendatory; that they were so meant by the States, and so understood by the Convention; and that the latter have accordingly planned and proposed a Constitution, which is to be of no more consequence than the paper on which it is written, unless it be stamped with the approbation of those to whom it is addressed. This reflection places the subject in a point of view altogether different, and will enable us to judge with propriety of the course taken by the Convention.

Let us view the ground on which the Convention stood.[4] It may be

---

[3] The reference is to Rhode Island, the one state that had refused to send delegates to the Federal Convention. (Editor)

[4] Madison referred to the calling of a convention by Virginia at Annapolis in September 1786 to deal with commercial matters. See note below. (Editor)

collected from their proceedings, that they were deeply and unanimously impressed with the crisis which had led their country almost with one voice to make so singular and solemn an experiment, for correcting the errors of a system by which this crisis had been produced; that they were no less deeply and unanimously convinced, that such a reform as they have proposed, was absolutely necessary to effect the purposes of their appointment. It could not be unknown to them, that the hopes and expectations of the great body of citizens, throughout this great empire, were turned with the keenest anxiety, to the event of their deliberations. They had every reason to believe that the contrary sentiments agitated the minds and bosoms of every external and internal foe to the liberty and prosperity of the United States. They had seen in the origin and progress of the experiment, the alacrity with which the *proposition* made by a single State (Virginia) towards a partial amendment of the confederation, had been attended to and promoted. They had seen the *liberty assumed* by a *very few* deputies, from a *very few* States, convened at Annapolis, of recommending a great and critical object, wholly foreign to their commission, not only justified by the public opinion, but actually carried into effect, by twelve out of the thirteen States.[5] They had seen in a variety of instances, assumptions by Congress, not only of recommendatory, but of operative powers, warranted in the public estimation, by occasions and objects infinitely less urgent than those by which their conduct was to be governed. They must have reflected, that in all great changes of established governments, forms ought to give way to substance; that a rigid adherence in such cases to the former, would render nominal and nugatory, the transcendent and precious right of the people to 'abolish or alter their governments as to them shall seem most likely to effect their Safety and Happiness;[6] since it is impossible for the people spontaneously and universally, to move in concert towards their object; and it is therefore essential, that such changes be instituted by some *informal and unauthorised propositions*, made by some patriotic and respectable citizen or number of citizens. They must have recollected that it was by this irregular and assumed privilege of proposing to the people plans for their safety and happiness, that the States were first united against the danger with which they were threatened by their ancient government; that Committees and Congresses, were formed for con-

[5]The Annapolis Convention had been called only to deal with the establishment of uniform commercial regulations. It resulted in a call to the several states to revise the Articles of Confederation. (Editor)

[6]*Declaration of Independence*. (Publius)

centrating their efforts, and defending their rights; and that *Conventions* were *elected* in *the several States*, for establishing the constitutions under which they are now governed; nor could it have been forgotten that no little ill-timed scruples, no zeal for adhering to ordinary forms, were any where seen, except in those who wished to indulge under these masks, their secret enmity to the substance contended for. They must have borne in mind, that as the plan to be framed and proposed, was to be submitted *to the people themselves*, the disapprobation of this supreme authority would destroy it for ever; its approbation blot out all antecedent errors and irregularities. It might even have occurred to them, that where a disposition to cavil prevailed, their neglect to execute the degree of power vested in them, and still more their recommendation of any measure whatever not warranted by their commission, would not less excite animadversion, than a recommendation at once of a measure fully commensurate to the national exigencies.

Had the Convention under all these impressions, and in the midst of all these considerations, instead of exercising a manly confidence in their country, by whose confidence they had been so peculiarly distinguished, and of pointing out a system capable in their judgment of securing its happiness, taken the cold and sullen resolution of disappointing its ardent hopes of sacrificing substance to forms, of committing the dearest interests of their country to the uncertainties of delay, and the hazard of events; let me ask the man, who can raise his mind to one elevated conception; who can awaken in his bosom, one patriotic emotion, what judgment ought to have been pronounced by the impartial world, by the friends of mankind, by every virtuous citizen, on the conduct and character of this assembly, or if there be a man whose propensity to condemn, is susceptible of no controul, let me then ask what sentence he has in reserve for the twelve States, who *usurped the power* of sending deputies to the Convention, a body utterly unknown to their constitutions; for Congress, who recommended the appointment of this body, equally unknown to the confederation; and for the State of New-York in particular, who first urged and then complied with this unauthorised interposition.[7]

But that the objectors may be disarmed of every pretext, it shall be granted for a moment, that the Convention were neither authorised by their commission, nor justified by circumstances, in proposing a Constitution for their country: Does it follow that the Constitution ought

---

[7]Madison presumably was referring to the memorial passed by the New York legislature in July 1782 calling on the Continental Congress to call a convention to consider amendments to the Articles of Confederation. (Editor)

for that reason alone to be rejected? If according to other noble precept it be lawful to accept good advice even from an enemy, shall we set the ignoble example of refusing such advice even when it is offered by our friends? The prudent enquiry in all cases, ought surely to be not so much *from whom* the advice comes, as whether the advice be *good*.

The sum of what has been here advanced and proved, is that the charge against the Convention of exceeding their powers, except in one instance little urged by the objectors, has no foundation to support it; that if they had exceeded their powers, they were not only warranted but required, as the confidential servants of their country, by the circumstances in which they were placed, to exercise the liberty which they assumed, and that finally, if they had violated both their powers, and their obligations in proposing a Constitution, this ought nevertheless to be embraced, if it be calculated to accomplish the views and happiness of the people of America. How far this character is due to the Constitution, is the subject under investigation.

Publius.

Appendix III

BALANCED BUDGET AMENDMENT PROPOSALS, 1987, BY U.S. SENATE AND HOUSE OF REPRESENTATIVES

100th CONGRESS
1st SESSION
S.J. RES. 50

Proposing an amendment to the Constitution of the United States to limit the expenditure of Government funds for any fiscal year to the projected revenue of the Government for that year and to limit the outstanding debt of the United States to thirty per centum of the projected gross national product.

IN THE SENATE OF THE UNITED STATES
February 5, 1987

JOINT RESOLUTION

Proposing an amendment to the Constitution of the United States to limit the expenditure of Government funds for any fiscal year to the projected revenue of the Government for that year and to limit the outstanding debt of the United States to thirty per centum of the projected gross national product.

Resolved by the Senate and House of Representatives of the United States of America in Congress assembled (two-thirds of each House concurring therein), That the following article is proposed as an amendment to the Constitution of the United States, which shall be valid to all intents and purposes as part of the Constitution when ratified by the legislatures of three-quarters of the several States within seven years from the date of its submission by the Congress:

"ARTICLE—

"SECTION 1. The total expenditure of the Government funds during any fiscal year shall not exceed the total revenue of the Government as projected by the Congress for that year.

"SECTION 2. The provisions of section 1 or 4, or both, shall not apply with respect to any fiscal year during any part of which the United States is in a state of war declared by the Congress pursuant to section 8 of article I of the Constitution or any fiscal year during which the Congress, by a vote of two-thirds of each House, adopts a joint resolution stating that a national emergency requires the suspension of the application of that section or sections. This joint resolution shall not be effective unless approved by the President.

"SECTION 3. The provisions of section 1 shall not apply with respect to any fiscal year for which the Congress projects that the real growth rate of the economy will be less than three per centum.

"SECTION 4. If the total expenditure of Government funds during any fiscal year exceeds the total revenue of the Government for that year because of section 3, the resulting deficit shall be extinguished by the end of the fifth fiscal year after the fiscal year in which that deficit occurs.

"SECTION 5. If the total revenue of the Government during any fiscal year exceeds the total expenditure of Government funds for that year, the resulting surplus shall be deemed revenue of the Government for the following fiscal year for purposes of this article.

"SECTION 6. As used in this article, expenditure of Government funds shall not include any expenditure for the redemption of bonds, notes, or other similar obligations of the Government, and revenue of the Government shall not include any revenue derived from the issuance of bonds, notes, or other similar obligations of the Government.

"SECTION 7. The Congress shall have power to enforce this article by appropriate legislation.

"SECTION 8. This article shall take effect on the first day of the third fiscal year beginning after the date of the ratification of this article."

100th CONGRESS
1st SESSION
H.J. RES. 184

Proposing an amendment to the Constitution to require that outlays of the United States in any fiscal year be no more than a certain percentage of the gross national product, and for other purposes.

IN THE HOUSE OF REPRESENTATIVES
March 11, 1987
Mr. Swindall introduced the following joint resolution, which was referred to the Committee on the Judiciary.

JOINT RESOLUTION

Proposing an amendment to the Constitution to require that outlays of the United States in any fiscal year be no more than a certain percentage of the gross national product, and for other purposes.

Resolved by the Senate and House of Representatives of the United States of America in Congress assembled (two-thirds of each House concurring therein), That the following article is proposed as an amendment to the Constitution of the United States, which shall be valid only if ratified by the legislatures of three-fourths of the several States within seven years after its submission to the States for ratification:

"ARTICLE—

"SECTION 1. (a) Except as provided in subsection (b), total outlays of the United States in any fiscal year—

"(1) shall not exceed 20 percent of the gross national product; and
"(2) shall not exceed total estimated receipts for that fiscal year.

"(b) For the first, second, and third fiscal years to which this article applies, total outlays of the United States shall not exceed 23 percent, 22 percent, and 21 percent, respectively, of the gross national product.
"(c) For purposes of determining the limitation under subsections (a)(1) and (b) for a fiscal year, the term 'gross national product' means an amount representing the market value of the Nation's output of goods and services, as determined by the President, during the most recent 12-month period (ending before the first day of such fiscal year) for which the President is able to determine such amount.

"SECTION 2. Congress may provide for a specific excess of outlays over the amount of outlays permitted for a fiscal year under section 1, but only if two-thirds of the entire membership of each House of Congress passes a bill directed solely to that subject and such bill becomes law.

"SECTION 3. Total receipts for any fiscal year set forth in the statement adopted under this article shall not increase, except as a result of an increase in national income during such fiscal year, unless two-thirds of the entire membership of each House of Congress passes a bill directed solely to approving specific additional receipts and such bill becomes law.

"SECTION 4. Before the beginning of each fiscal year, the President shall transmit to Congress a proposed statement of receipts and outlays for that year consistent with the provision of this article.

"SECTION 5. For purposes of this article, total receipts includes all receipts of the United States except those derived from borrowing, and total outlays includes all outlays of the United States except those for repayment of debt principle.

"SECTION 6. Congress may waive the provisions of this article for any fiscal year for which a declaration of war by Congress is in effect.

"SECTION 7. Congress may enforce this article by appropriate legislation.

"SECTION 8. This article shall apply with respect to the second fiscal year beginning after ratification of this article and to each succeeding fiscal year."

100th CONGRESS
1st SESSION
S.J. RES. 112

Proposing an amendment to the Constitution of the United States which requires (except during time of war and subject to suspension by the Congress) that the total amount of money expended by the United States during any fiscal year not exceed the amount of certain revenue received by the United States during such fiscal year and not exceed 20 per centum of the gross national product of the United States during the previous calendar year.

IN THE SENATE OF THE UNITED STATES
April 9 (legislative day, MARCH 30), 1987
MR. SHELBY introduced the following joint resolution; which was read twice referred to the Committee on the Judiciary.

JOINT RESOLUTION

Proposing an amendment to the Constitution of the United States which requires (except during time of war and subject to suspension by the Congress) that the total amount of money expended by the United states during any fiscal year not exceed the amount of certain revenue received by the United States during such fiscal year and not exceed 20 per centum of the gross national product of the United States during the previous calendar year.

Resolved by the Senate and House of Representatives of the United States of America in Congress assembled (two-thirds of each House concurring therein), That the following article is proposed as an amendment to the Constitution of the United States, to be valid only if ratified by the legislatures of three-fourths of the several States within seven years of the date of final passage of this joint resolution:

"ARTICLE—

"SECTION 1. The total amount of money expended by the United States in any fiscal year of the Treasury of the United States (or other similar period of time designated by the Congress for purposes of accounts, receipts, expenditures, estimates, and appropriations) shall not exceed the total amount of revenue received by the United States during such fiscal year, except revenue received from the issuance of bonds, notes, or other obligations of the United States.

"SECTION 2. The total amount of money expended by the United States in any fiscal year of the Treasury of the United States (or other similar period of time designated by the Congress for purposes of accounts, receipts, expenditures, estimates, and appropriations) shall not exceed the amount equal to 20 per centum of the gross national product of the United States during the last calendar year ending before the beginning of such fiscal year.

"SECTION 3. Sections 1 and 2 of this Article shall not apply during any fiscal year of the Treasury of the United States (or other similar period) during any part of which the United States is at war as declared by the Congress under section 8 of Article I of the Constitution.

"SECTION 4. Sections 1 and 2 of this Article may be suspended by a concurrent resolution approved by a vote of a majority of the Members of each House of the Congress. Any suspension of sections 1 and 2 of this Article under this section shall be effective only during the fiscal year of the Treasury of the United States (or other similar period) during which such suspension is approved.

"SECTION 5. This Article shall take effect on the first day of the first fiscal year of the Treasury of the United States (or similar period) beginning after the date of the adoption of this Article.

"SECTION 6. The Congress shall have power to enforce this Article by appropriate legislation."

Appendix IV

TABULATION OF ARTICLE V APPLICATIONS SINCE 1789

Twenty Categories of Applications:

STATE	TOTALS BY STATE	MISC.	TAX OR MUNI. BOND PROHIBIT STATE	FREEDOM OF CHOICE OF SCHOOLS	REVENUE SHARING	PRESIDENTIAL DISABILITY & SUCCESSION	REDISTRIB. OF PRES. ELECTORS	PRAYER IN SCHOOLS	COURT OF THE UNION	APPORTIONMENT	SUPREME COURT DECISIONS	EXCLUSIVE STATE JURISDICTION OVER SCHOOLS	REVISION OF ARTICLE V	TREATY MAKING	PRESIDENTIAL TENURE LIMIT	WORLD FEDERAL GOVERNMENT	LIMITATION OF FED. TAXING; REPEAL 16TH AMEND.	REPEAL OF PROHIBITION 21ST AMEND.	ANTI- POLYGAMY	DIRECT ELECTION OF SENATORS	GENERAL
ALABAMA	8	3			1				1	2							1				
ALASKA	1									1											
ARIZONA	2							1		1											
ARKANSAS	11	1			1		1			2	1		1				1			3	
CALIFORNIA	9	3								1	1		1							3	
COLORADO	7	1					1		1	2							1			1	
CONNECTICUT	3	1														1	1				
DELAWARE	3															1	1		1		
FLORIDA	12	1			1	1						3				3	1		1		1
GEORGIA	9		1		2				1		1		1	1					1		1
HAWAII	1				1																
IDAHO	9	2								2			2							2	1
ILLINOIS	14	1					1			2		1	2	1			1		1	3	1
INDIANA	9	1								2			1		1	1	2		1		
IOWA	10	1			1					1			1				2			4	
KANSAS	9									2			1				1		1	4	
KENTUCKY	5									1			1							1	2
LOUISIANA	13	2	1	1	2						1						2		1	1	2
MAINE	6				1												2		1	1	1
MARYLAND	6				1					1							1	1	2		
MASSACHUSETTS	6	3		1				1										1	1		
MICHIGAN	7			1				1					1		1		1		1	1	
MINNESOTA	4									1			1				2				

168

Table of applications by state and subject (subject column headings not shown on this page; columns identified by their subject totals in the final row). Page 169.

State																						Total
MISSISSIPPI	1				1							1						2			2	7
MISSOURI		3			1				1			2			1						1	8
MONTANA		6	1		1							2			1	1					1	13
NEBRASKA		4	1	1	1							1			1							9
NEVADA		6	1		1							3					1					12
NEW HAMPSHIRE			1		2							1										5
NEW JERSEY	1	1	1	1	1	1						1									1	7
NEW MEXICO			1		1																	2
NEW YORK	1	1	1	1		1						1									2	5
NORTH CAROLINA	1	2			1							1			1							5
NORTH DAKOTA		1	1								1	2					2					6
OHIO	1	2	1																			6
OKLAHOMA	1	1	1		1				1			2			1		1			1	1	8
OREGON	1	6	1		1																1	10
PENNSYLVANIA		1	2		1							1			1						1	5
RHODE ISLAND					1																	4
SOUTH CAROLINA	1		1		1				1			2	1		1							7
SOUTH DAKOTA		3	1		1				3			2			1					1	1	12
TENNESSEE		4	1		1							1			1	1		1		1		9
TEXAS	1	2	1		1				2			2			1	1	1				3	15
UTAH		1			1							2										5
VERMONT			1													1				1		1
VIRGINIA	2	1			1				1	1		2			1						1	10
WASHINGTON	1	1	2									1										5
WEST VIRGINIA			1												1		1					2
WISCONSIN	2	3	1	1	1							1			1						1	11
WYOMING		1			2				1			1										7
TOTAL APPLICATIONS BY SUBJECT	18	75	30	5	42	8	5	3	19	6	4	54	5	4	11	3	21	7	2	4	36	356

169

SELECTED BIBLIOGRAPHY

ARTICLES

Albert, Lee A. "Justiciability and Theories of Judicial Review: A Remote Relationship." *Southern California Law Review* 50 (1977):1139.

Black, Charles L., Jr. "Amending the Constitution: A Letter to a Congressman." *Yale Law Journal* 82 (1972):189.

Bowers, Claude G. "Jefferson and the Bill of Rights." *Virginia Law Review* 41 (1955):709.

Buckwalter, Doyle W. "Constitutional Conventions and State Legislators." *Journal of Public Law* 20 (1971):543.

Congressional Quarterly, 1985–88.

Corwin, Edward S., and Mary Louise Ramsey. "The Constitutional Law of Constitutional Amendment." *Notre Dame Law Review* 26 (1951):185.

Dellinger, Walter E. "Constitutional Politics: A Rejoinder." *Harvard Law Review* 97 (1983):466.

———. "The Legitimacy of Constitutional Change: Rethinking the Amendment Process." *Harvard Law Review* 97 (1983):386.

———. "The Recurring Question of the 'Limited' Constitutional Convention." *Yale Law Journal* 88 (1979):623.

Gilliam, Thomas A. "Constitutional Conventions: Precedents, Problems, and Proposals." *St. Louis University Law Journal* (1971).

Goldberg, Arthur. "The Proposed Constitutional Convention." *Hastings Law Quarterly* 11 (1983):1.

Graham, Fred P. "The Role of the States in Proposing Constitutional

Amendments." *American Bar Association Journal* 49 (December 1963):1175.

Gunther, Gerald. "Constitutional Brinkmanship: Stumbling Toward a Convention." *American Bar Association Journal* 65 (1979):1046.

Hajdu, Robert, and Bruce E. Rosenblum. "The Process of Constitutional Amendment" (Note). *Columbia Law Review* 79 (1979):106.

Healy, Linda C. "Past and Present Convention Calls: From Gay Abandon to Cautious Resistance." Paper presented at Southern Political Science Association Meeting, Savannah, GA, November 1, 1984.

Heller, Francis H. "Limiting a Constitutional Convention: The State Precedents." *Cardozo Law Review* 3 (1982):563.

Henkin, Louis. "Is There a 'Political Question' Doctrine?" *Yale Law Journal* 85 (1976):597.

Kay, Richard S. "The Creation of Constitutions in Canada and the United States." *Canada-United States Law Journal* III (1984):120.

Lowi, Theodore. "Toward Functionalism in Political Science: The Case of Innovation in Party Systems," *American Political Science Review* 57 (1963):570.

Marsh, James G., and John P. Olson. "The New Institutionalism: Organizational Factors in Political Life," *American Political Science Review* 78 (1984):734.

Martin, Philip L. "The Application Clause of Article Five," *Political Science Quarterly* 85 (1970):616.

Martineau, Robert J. "The Mandatory Referendum on Calling a State Constitutional Convention: Enforcing the People's Right to Reform Their Government," *Ohio State Law Journal* 31 (1970):421.

Noonan, John T., Jr. "The Convention Method of Constitutional Amendment: Its Meaning, Usefulness and Wisdom." *Congressional Record*, 3 May 1979, p. S9841.

Note. *Harvard Journal of Legislation* 11 (1973):127.

Note. "Proposed Legislation on the Convention Method of Amending the United States Constitution." *Harvard Law Review* 85 (1972):1612.

Parenti, Michael. "The Constitution as an Elitist Document." In Robert A. Goldwin and William A. Schambra, eds. *How Democratic Is the Constitution?* Washington, DC: American Enterprise Institute, 1980.

Saulnier, Raymond J. "Do We Need a Balanced-Budget Amendment to the Constitution?" *Presidential Studies Quarterly* 28 (Winter 1988):157.

Schrag, Philip G. "By the People: The Political Dynamics of a Constitutional Convention." *Georgia Law Journal* 72 (1984):819.

"Should a Constitutional Amendment Be Adopted to Require Balanced Federal Budget?" *Congressional Digest*, May 1979, pp. 138–159.

Smith, Edward P. "The Movement Toward a Second Constitutional Convention in 1788." In J. Franklin Jameson, ed. *Essays in the Constitutional History of the United States in the Formative Period 1775–1789*. Boston: Houghton Mifflin, 1889.

"State Action Toward a Constitutional Convention." *Congressional Digest*, May 1979, p. 134.

Sturm, Albert L. and Janice C. May. "State Constitutions and Constitutional Revision: 1986–87." In *The Book of States 1988–89*, Vol. 27. Lexington, KY: Council of State Governments, 1988.

Tribe, Laurence. "A Constitution We Are Amending: In Defense of a Restrained Judicial Role." *Harvard Law Review* 97 (1983):433.

———. "Issues Raised by Requesting Congress to Call a Constitutional Convention to Propose a Balanced Budget Amendment." *Pacific Law Journal* 10 (1979):627.

Weber, Paul J. "The Constitutional Convention: A Safe Political Option." *The Journal of Law and Politics* 3 (Winter 1986):57.

———. "Madison's Opposition to a Second Convention." *Polity* 20 (Spring 1988):91.

BOOKS

Abraham, Henry J. *Freedom and the Court: Civil Rights and Liberties in the United States*. 5th ed. New York: Oxford University Press, 1988.

———. *The Judicial Process: An Introductory Analysis of the Courts of the United States, England, and France*. 5th ed. New York: Oxford University Press, 1986.

———. *Justices and Presidents: A Political History of Appointments to the Supreme Court*. 2nd ed. New York: Oxford University Press, 1985.

Allen, Tip H., and Coleman B. Ransone, Jr. *Constitutional Revision in Theory and Practice*. University: Bureau of Public Administration, University of Alabama, 1962.

American Bar Association. Special Constitutional Convention Study Committee. *Amendment of the Constitution by the Convention Method Under Article V*. Chicago: 1974.

American Enterprise Institute for Public Policy Research. "A Constitutional Convention: How Well Would it Work?" Transcript of a forum held 23 May 1979.

———. *A Convention to Amend the Constitution?* Washington, DC: American Enterprise Institute for Public Policy Research, 1967.

———. *Proposals for a Constitutional Convention to Require a Balanced Budget.* Washington, DC: American Enterprise Institute for Public Policy Research, 1979.

Ames, Herman V. *Proposed Amendments to the Constitution of the United States During the First Century of Its History.* Reprint. New York: Burt Franklin, 1970.

Beard, Charles. *An Economic Interpretation of the Constitution.* New York: Macmillan, 1935.

Berry, Jeffrey R. *The Interest Group Society.* Boston: Little, Brown and Co., 1984.

Caplan, Russell L. *Constitutional Brinkmanship: Amending the Constitution by National Convention.* New York: Oxford University Press, 1988.

Cardozo, Benjamin N. *The Nature of the Judicial Process.* New Haven: Yale University Press, 1921.

Cebula, Richard J. *Federal Budget Deficits: An Economic Analysis.* Lexington, MA: Lexington Books, 1987.

Cornwell, Elmer E., Jr., Jay S. Goodman, and Wayne R. Swanson. *Constitutional Conventions: The Politics of Revision.* New York: National Municipal League, 1974.

Downs, Anthony. *An Economic Theory of Democracy.* Boston: Little, Brown, and Co., 1957.

Edel, Wilbur. *A Constitutional Convention: Threat or Challenge?* New York: Praeger, 1981.

Eisner, Robert. *How Real is the Federal Deficit?* New York: The Free Press, 1986.

Elder, Shirley and Norman Ornstein. *Interest Groups, Lobbying and Policymaking.* Washington, DC: Congressional Quarterly Press, 1978.

Eldersveld, Samuel James. *Political Parties in American Society.* New York: Basic Books, 1982.

Elliot, Jonathan, ed. *Debates in the Several State Conventions on the Adoption of the Federal Constitution, As Recommended by the General Convention at Philadelphia in 1787.* New York: Burt Franklin Reprints, 1974.

Farrand, Max, ed. *The Records of the Federal Convention of 1787,* rev. ed. New Haven: Yale University Press, 1966.

Fink, Richard H. and Jack C. High, eds. *A Nation in Debt: Economists Debate the Federal Budget Deficit.* Frederick, MD: University Publications of America, 1987.

Graves, W. Brooke, ed. *Major Problems in State Constitutional Revision.* Westport, CT: Greenwood Press, 1960.

Grossman, Joel B., and Richard S. Wells. *Constitutional Law and Judicial Policy Making.* 3rd ed. New York: Longman, 1988.

Hall, Kermit, Harold M. Hyman, and Leon V. Sigal, eds. *The Constitutional Convention as an Amending Device.* Washington, DC: APSA and AHA, 1981.

Hennessy, Bernard C. *Public Opinion,* 2nd ed. Belmont, CA: Wadsworth Publishing Co., 1970.

Hume, David. *Enquiries Concerning Human Understanding and Concerning the Principles of Morals.* 3d. ed. New York: Oxford University Press, 1975.

Hunt, Gaillard, ed. *The Writings of James Madison,* Vols. I–IX. New York: G. P. Putnam's Sons, 1900–1910.

Jameson, John Alexander. *A Treatise on Constitutional Conventions, Their History, Powers, and Modes of Proceeding,* 4th ed. Chicago: Callaghan and Co., 1887.

Key, V. O., Jr. *Public Opinion and American Democracy.* New York: Knopf Publishers, 1961.

McLaughlin, Andrew C. *The Confederation and the Constitution, 1783–1789.* New York: Crowell-Collier, 1962.

Miller, Arthur S. *The Secret Constitution and the Need for Constitutional Change.* Westport, CT: Greenwood Press, 1987.

Moore, W. S., and Rudolph G. Penner. *The Constitution and the Budget.* Washington, DC: American Enterprise Institute for Public Policy Research, 1980.

Morris, Richard B. *Witnesses at the Creation.* New York: New American Library, 1985.

Olson, Mancur, Jr. *The Logic of Collective Action.* Cambridge: Harvard University Press, 1965.

Peterson, Merrill D., ed. *Democracy, Liberty, and Property, The State Constitutional Conventions of the 1820s.* New York: Bobbs-Merrill, 1966.

Rossiter, Clinton. *1787: The Grand Convention.* New York: Macmillan, 1966.

Rutland, Robert A., and Charles F. Hobson, eds. *The Papers of James Madison.* Charlottesville: University Press of Virginia, 1977.

Salisbury, Robert, ed. *Interest Group Politics in America.* New York: Harper & Row, 1970.

Schrag, Philip G. *Behind the Scenes: The Politics of a Constitutional Convention.* Washington, DC: Georgetown University Press, 1985.

Sommers, Albert T., ed. *Reconstructing the Federal Budget: A Trillion Dollar Quandary.* New York: Praeger, 1984.

Storing, Herbert. *The Anti-Federalist: Writings by the Opponents of the Constitution.* Chicago: University of Chicago Press, 1986.

Sturm, Albert L. *Thirty Years of State Constitution-Making: 1938–1968.* New York: National Municipal League, 1970.

Wheeler, John P. *The Constitutional Convention: A Manual on Its Planning, Organization, and Operation.* New York: National Municipal League, 1961.

———, ed. *Salient Issues of Constitutional Revision.* New York: National Municipal League, 1961.

Wildavsky, Aaron. *The Politics of the Budgetary Process*, 4th ed. Boston: Little, Brown, 1984.

CONGRESSIONAL MATERIALS

Documents Illustrative of the Formation of the Union of the American States. H.R. Doc. No. 398, 69th Cong., 1st Sess., 1927.

Hearing on Constitutional Convention Procedures Before the Subcomm. on the Constitution of the Senate Comm. on the Judiciary, 96th Cong., 1st Sess., 29 Nov. 1979.

INDEX

About the Authors

PAUL J. WEBER is professor and chairman of the Department of Political Science at the University of Louisville, Kentucky. He wrote *Private Churches and Public Money* (Greenwood Press, 1981) and contributed to numerous publications including *The Review of Politics, Polity, The Journal of Law and Politics*, and several law reviews.

BARBARA A. PERRY is an assistant professor of Political Science at Sweet Briar College. She has written articles for the *Journal of Church and State* and the *Journal of Law and Politics* and is at work on another book regarding the U.S. Supreme Court's "Catholic Seat."